Y0-BCS-347

WORD AND SPIRIT

WORD
AND
SPIRIT

a monastic review

5

Christology

ST. BEDE'S PUBLICATIONS
Still River, Massachusetts

BT
202
.C45
1983

Copyright © 1983 by St. Bede's Publications
All Rights Reserved
PRINTED IN THE UNITED STATES OF AMERICA

Published with ecclesiastical permission

Articles appearing in this journal are abstracted and indexed in *Religious and Theological Abstracts*. They are also indexed by *RIC*, the *Bibliographical Repertory of Christian Institutions*, published by Cerdic Publications in France.

LIBRARY OF CONGRESS CATALOGING IN PUBLICATION DATA

Main entry under title:

Christology.

  (Word & spirit, ISSN 0193-9211 ; 5)
  Includes bibliographical references.
  Contents: Christology from above and Christology from below / Louis Bouyer — Christ in the Rule of Benedict / Martin Cawley — What Christ means to me / Felicitas Corrigan — [etc.]
  1. Jesus Christ—Person and offices—Addresses, essays, lectures. I. Series: Word and spirit ; 5.
BX801.W67 vol. 5 [BT202]   282s [232]   83-4420
ISBN 0-932506-28-3

CONTENTS

PREFACE

WORD AND SPIRIT is a monastic review published once a year, focusing on scriptural, theological and spiritual themes, or commemorating the anniversary of a significant event in the history of Christianity. Bringing together the work of scholars from all over the world, it offers important insights in its conspectus of man's remarkable religious heritage.

*   *   *

The 1983 issue of *Word and Spirit* has been prepared to celebrate this Holy Year which marks the 1950th anniversary of the death and Resurrection of Our Lord Jesus Christ. The theme is Christology and each of the authors, whether writing from a theological or from a more personal viewpoint, offers a stimulating study of some aspect of the subject.

THIS ISSUE:

In honor of this Holy Year which was declared by the Holy Father in memory of the death and Resurrection of Christ, we present this issue of *Word and Spirit* on Christology. The authors take up various aspects of the theme —some discussing theological questions centered on the person of Jesus Christ; some looking at the way Christ is presented to us in Scripture or in the liturgy; and still others discussing their own experience of Him in different areas of their lives. We invite our readers to share these articles and to reflect seriously on their own personal experience of Christ as the Word of God in their lives so they too can more fully answer Our Lord's question to each of us: "Who do *you* say that I am?"

Focusing on the modern debates surrounding the person of Jesus Christ, *Hans Urs von Balthasar* sees Him as the Word whose activity cannot be separated from His message. He further explains that all theology concerning God, Christ, the Church, and man and the world, remains nothing but an approach to the Word and the Spirit within Him.

Louis Bouyer calls the traditional definition of Christ produced by the Church "Christology from above" and discusses the need to develop a "Christology from below" starting from the fact that Christ was a complete man, *the* Son of God, and only as such can be seen as making God real for us, and bringing us also to be true sons of God through Him.

Looking at Salvation history in relation to Creation history, *Luc Richard* faces the problematic of how Christ can be both Creator and created, and answers the question by seeing in Jesus Christ the revelation of the right relation between Creator and Creation.

Colman O'Neill looks at the words of Our Lord at the Last Supper and their meaning for us, explaining that Redemption is a work of divine love, calling up sacrifice in the person of Christ only in order that it might be created as well in the hearts of all who accept this mystery.

The Philippians hymn (2:5-11) is the subject of *Stanley Marrow's* study. He discusses recent scholarship on the "hymn," but sees it as a necessary part of the Letter, stating both the foundation and the principle of Christian life in Christ.

Jean Leclercq defines Christ as the contemplator par excellence, and states that all experience of prayer and of contemplation is a participation in the experience of Jesus who is "the contemplator of the Father in the Spirit for the Church"; and when we participate in His contemplation we participate in His mission of salvation for the Church.

Going back to the Christ of the Scriptures, *Jean Gribomont* concerns himself with the early Christological development in the East and its relationship to the flowering of monastic life. Then, turning our eyes to the West, *Martin Cawley* devotes himself to the names of Christ in the Rule of Benedict, studying the care with which Benedict alludes to Christ and the various perspectives which are orientated toward Him.

In an attempt to guide the reader in forming his own Christology, *William Meninger* stresses that we must look at our own experiences of Christ in the light of Scripture, and the Church's response to Scripture, as well as to other interpretative elements which come from our tradition and society. Each one's Christology will be different but should be developed as a continuing process through prayer and as a response to grace.

Examples of forming one's own personal Christology are given by our last two articles. *Felicitas Corrigan* shares her own thoughts with us and gives a good example of how we encounter Christ in Scripture, liturgy, and in our everyday experience, while *Basil Pennington* suggests that, to develop a personal Christology, we turn to prayer and *lectio divina* in order to experience God himself, and then share this living faith with others.

WORD AND SPIRIT

BASIC CHRISTOLOGICAL QUESTIONS

Hans Urs von Balthasar

*(Priest-theologian from
Basel, Switzerland)*

1. The Preaching of Jesus

The philosopher, Hegel, once commented in a brief note
that the events of Jesus' history were forever receding
further into the past and so his teaching would, in common
parlance, "soon not be true anymore." Wanting to arrest
this recession, Hegel took the historical life, death and
resurrection of Jesus, elaborated from it a general law
governing all being and extolled Jesus' destiny as the highest symbolic representation of this law. But if we look
at the general spiritual state of our world, seemingly so
secularized, it gives no support whatever to the prophecy
that Jesus' history would "soon not be true anymore." No
book comes near to being so much in demand, so much
discussed and so assiduously commented as the Bible, and
especially the New Testament. The debate concerning
Jesus continues, more passionate than ever, whether we
think of the disputes within the Church or in ecumenism
or with Judaism and Islam or in the area of liberation
theology where the spiritual fate of Latin America is being
decided. Let the world pose as worldly as it will, the fact
remains Jesus is more present to it than anyone else.

Still, it might be claimed that since the Enlightenment,
there has been so much debate within the Church about
what the Gospels mean, that the earlier, uniform picture
of Jesus has been pulled to pieces to such an extent that
sheer biblical criticism has rendered it hardly recognizable
for many unsettled minds among the faithful, and the
champions of Jesus' cause have the air of a body inexorably

destroying itself from within. So it might seem. Yet in some strange, inexplicable fashion the portrait of the Nazarene, which had apparently been shattered for good and all, emerges whole and entire. Two inseparable forces are responsible for this miracle: the Word and the Spirit within it. A whole succession of critical theories, assaulting the word of the Gospels one after another, have gone their way and perished. The Word and the Holy Spirit within it still stand: "Heaven and earth and all biblical criticism will pass away, but my words will not pass away." We are speaking here, of course, only of destructive criticism, not of the kind of scientific study of the biblical text which can so usefully enrich our understanding of it.

We will attempt, in four brief sections, to cast light on the central area of the modern debate. These are questions which not only rouse the academics, they spill over into the world of the non-professionals and finally find their way into popular literature where, in the form of slogans, they are bandied about in triumph and unsettle many a believer. We will deal first with the preaching of the historical Jesus, then with the post-resurrection presentation of this teaching; thirdly with Jesus' self-consciousness, especially in relation to the approach of the passion, and finally with whether or not he founded a church. These themes are all intimately linked and as we turn to the first we shall immediately find ourselves at the heart of the problem.

*   *   *

There is no doubt that when Jesus began to preach he had a single, central theme: the Kingdom of God is near, close at hand, imminent. His opening words in Mark summarize all he is going to say in the future: "The time is fulfilled, and the Kingdom of God is at hand; repent, and believe in the gospel" (Mk. 1:15). The good news, the Gospel, is precisely that the kingdom of God is near. The Baptist had also issued a call to penance but it had been in the light of a coming, final judgment of God. For Jesus the object of a man's conversion is that, instead of judgment of sin, there will be for him the good news: God's kingdom is at hand and you are invited to enter it. There is, too, another difference between the message of Jesus and that of the Baptist: the latter pointed forward to something greater, something before which he could only give way, while Jesus, on the contrary, his word, his activity, his whole being, are quite inseparable from his message. He is not merely entrusted with proclaiming that the kingdom is imminent; rather, its very imminence can be apprehended only in him, indeed is only *had* in him. In the same first chapter of Mark "they were all amazed, so that they questioned among themselves, saying, 'What is this? A new teaching! Delivered with authority...' " (Mk. 1:27). What was new and filled them with amazement was precisely the authority seen and sensed in Jesus' teaching and behavior. The indissoluble connection between the proclamation of the kingdom and the person of Jesus is evidenced in every Gospel pericope; it is impossible to find a single passage that contradicts it. We need not invoke such obvious instances as those in the Sermon on the Mount where Jesus, expounding the word of God, goes beyond the ancient content of the Law and declares: "You have heard that it was said...but I say to you...."

But if the kingdom of God and Jesus form such a unity, why does he speak of the kingdom as something no more than imminent? Why does he not simply say, "I myself am the kingdom"? We are dealing with a mystery. In one sense, indeed, the kingdom could be described as present; so Jesus can say: "If it is by the Spirit of God that I cast out demons, then the kingdom of God has come upon you" (Mt. 12:28). But in that case why talk of an approaching kingdom? The plain answer is, because Jesus himself is still approaching. He is like a word that is incomprehensible so long as it is unfinished. He is, in fact, a trisyllabic word:

life-death-resurrection. Only after the third syllable—the
resurrection—will the disciples be able to understand the
whole word, and then at last the kingdom will no longer be
near but present and completely so.

Now the central teaching of John's Gospel, Jesus as the
Word of God, suddenly makes sense. In the Old Testament
God spoke many words, but in Jesus the Word becomes
flesh, that is, human. His preaching, work, suffering, and
humanity make up the comprehensive conclusive word
God has to say to us. All earlier utterances maintain their
truth within that Word but the man Jesus *is* the one Word,
making all things new, giving everything a wonderful,
transcendent and unexpectedly coherent meaning. Reading John we are now able to understand why Jesus proclaims not himself but the kingdom of the God whom he
also calls his Father. He is not just any word; a prophetic
word about God. He is the Word in whom God manifests
himself. No human word says anything about itself; it does
not proclaim itself but something else. It has a content.
That is why Jesus can say: "If I bear witness to myself, my
testimony is not true" (Jn. 5:31). More than any human
word he proclaims something, Someone, the Father to
whose service his whole being is dedicated. "For I have
come down from heaven, not to do my own will, but the
will of him who sent me" (Jn. 6:38). Yet at the same time
this Word which proclaims the kingdom of the Father is, as
we have seen, inseparable from its content. If, as Hans
Küng would have it, Jesus were no more than God's
"agent" in the world, then we could indeed make a separation. But in the Gospel, all four Gospels, the content—
kingdom and Father—has no other vessel to contain it than
the Word, the Son. And so with penetrating logic Jesus
says: "My teaching is not mine but his who sent me" (Jn.
7:16). The One who speaks and the Word spoken are in one
another, and in one another in an unique, incomparable
way that cannot be equated with any other relationship

between God and man: "He who sees me sees him who sent me" (Jn. 12:45). To talk of Jesus' "cause" is misleading, for while the Father, who dwells and acts within him, is certainly his prime concern, he is not his "cause."

John merely spells out something already present in the synoptics and in the earliest strata of Jesus' preaching. Jesus demands faith in himself from the very start. How then could someone who does not believe in him understand his concern with the Father or understand Jesus himself? How can even a believer grasp that here he is being given a quite new, unprecedented sight of the living God? What becomes visible is so dazzling that Judaism and Islam recoil in horror as from something supremely scandalous: God not only in heaven but as a man on earth! And God not only as Speaker and Speech, Father and Son, but also as Spirit; their mutual, free, personal Love bestowed as gift on the world; God as triune Love, completely self-contained, manifested to the world by the sending of his Son and the Son's surrender of himself to death for us all. Implicit or explicit, the dogma of the triune God and the redemption of the world runs through the whole New Testament; it is embodied in the very being of Jesus who speaks to the eternal Father with no less reverence than authority, and has resting on him the eternal Spirit of God whom he both obeys and bestows on others.

2. The Church's Presentation of Jesus

What we have just said provides us with the essential answer to the various objections leveled at the seemingly arbitrary interpretation of Jesus' words by the post-resurrection community. Put neatly, the chief objection runs as follows: the preacher becomes the one preached, that is, the one who proclaimed not himself but only the kingdom of God, has become the center of the confession of faith: Jesus Christ, the Son of God, Savior of the world, consubstantial with the Father, true God and true Man in one Person....

But if, as we said, the kingdom of God proclaimed by Jesus was inseparable from his own person; if the fulfillment of his destiny—by crucifixion and resurrection—fulfilled his proclamation; if the kingdom that had been near at hand had now at last come and was present within him; then why should he not become the object of the Church's own proclamation? And in any case the Church's proclamation was in no way confined to the person of Jesus but embraced the whole God, with Jesus now seen and conceived as his visible epiphany. Jesus himself proclaimed the kingdom of God; of that very God whom Israel knew as its Creator and the Lord of its covenant, and whom Jesus called his Father in a quite new and unique sense: his "Papa," Abba; that same Father, too, who gives his Holy Spirit to all who ask him for it (Lk. 11:13). This was God possessed, indeed, of all the best and most vivid characteristics of the Old Testament covenant God (there was no danger of Jesus' contemporaries not knowing about whom he was talking), but radiant now with characteristics greater in depth and inciting greater wonder, thrown into relief by the human life and conduct of Jesus himself. He formulated no dogma about God but he showed forth by his life that God is Three-in-one and infinitely loving towards the world. The kingdom he proclaimed was no recondite abstraction. It stood out vivid and concrete in his portrayal of the mind of the Father and the action of the Spirit. This was the merciful Father, whom we can and should imitate; who lets his sun rise on the good and the evil. This was the Father who forgives, if we take his Spirit upon ourselves and forgive those in debt to us. Whoever has the mind to love is, as Jesus says to the scribe, "not far from the Kingdom of God" (Mk. 12:34).

Thus, after all, the Church only appropriated Jesus' own proclamation to proclaim it in that completeness

now attained through the cross and Easter and to speak
explicitly of Jesus where before he had only remained
implicit within the teaching about God. In the preaching of
the apostles, the principal agent is still the Father, who,
through Jesus' incarnation, death and resurrection proclaims to the world its reconciliation now achieved. And
looking ahead to an apparently late document such as the
First Letter of John, we see that the same still holds, the
thesis being that God is love and the proof none other than
that God gave up his only Son for the world, for us, as is
attested by the Spirit we received from him. The Church
does not proclaim Jesus in isolation but the God of love,
whose love is shown by the fact that he did not surrender
just any person to death, not any "agent"—what good
would that have done the world?—but that divine Son
who was alone capable of winning pardon for the world's
guilt. The synoptics, Paul and John were all unanimous on
this.

This is why it became essential to establish the true
divinity of the man Jesus. The Church contested for this
truth right into the fourth century in both her theology
and her Councils. Everything, indeed, depended on it. The
process of formulation was a lengthy one and specific
Greek terms were used by the Councils to safeguard the
truth. This has occasioned talk of a Hellenization of the
Christian faith, but the truth is the complete opposite. It
was a liberation from the Greek philosophical concept of
God where only one, God the Father, could count as the
supreme, true God, with Son and Spirit necessarily nothing
but subordinate powers. The Councils which developed
Christology, and in so doing protected the Trinitarian
mystery against Greek rationalism, were simply defending
the integrity of the New Testament. In John the Jews
persecute Jesus "for blasphemy; because you, being a man,
make yourself God" (Jn. 10:33). There could hardly be a
clearer formulation of the real claim of Jesus' entire life.

Whether and how Jesus himself defined his own dignity
is of no importance. Certainly he did not want to be openly
acknowleged as Messiah; there were too many misconceptions about this abroad. It is highly probable that he called
himself "the Son of man," but the precise connotation he
gave the title is controverted and perhaps we shall never
know exactly what it was. It is possible that on occasion he
described himself as "the Son." This was for long referred
to late Greek influence but has now been clearly proved to
derive from Old Testament concepts. And we must always
remember that the dignity radiating from Jesus' whole
person required no title for it to be universally acknowledged by friend and foe alike. The titles assigned him by
the Church's preaching were simply true and correct
designations of his identity.

Then again Jesus, being an infinite mystery, could
not possibly have been summed up in a single formula.
A variety of Christological statements approached the
mystery from different angles. There is so little contradiction in these statements that it is foolish to construct
out of them a Christological pluralism which would render
impossible any Church teaching. It is clear that the exaltation of Christ from the status of God's servant to that of
Lord of the world in no way contradicts the fact that when
in abasement, in kenosis, he was already the Son of God.
One cannot *become* God unless one already *is* God.

As regards the Church's self-understanding, she stood
and still stands confronted by the deep mystery of her
origin. Inasmuch as Jesus is Israel's Messiah, God's new
and eternal covenant is not another covenant alongside the
one with Israel but rather its fulfillment, solemnly foretold
by the prophets. But insofar as Jesus was more than a
merely human Messiah, and the New Covenant established in his sacrifice, his flesh and blood, the Church's
reality, in Paul's words, surpasses its Jewish model as the
substance the shadow (Col. 2:17; Heb. 8:5). All theology

concerning God, Christ, the Church, her sacraments, and finally, man and the world, remains nothing but an approach to the Word who in the beginning was with God, who himself was God, who became flesh and in whom God has manifested himself, giving grace upon grace. How good it is that this living Word remains eternally greater than anything we can master by words and concepts! All the Church's meditating and discoursing upon God is never anything but an invitation to pray, to prostrate in adoration and, by adoring, to acknowledge that God's majesty and merciful condescension are always greater than we can ever grasp.

3. Jesus' Self-Consciousness

Guardini was certainly right in repeatedly insisting that we cannot make a study of Jesus' psyche, yet the theologians, indeed any believer, cannot avoid the question concerning the self-consciousness of Jesus. One realizes this on reading recent exegetical works which claim to be able to establish that Jesus knew next to nothing of his approaching death on the cross (the predictions being later additions) and, even when he did recognize it as inevitable, never said and therefore never knew anything about its saving power for Israel, let alone for the whole world.

Such a thesis is, of course, in flat contradiction to the text of the Gospels, where we find Jesus on several important occasions, predicting not only his death but also his resurrection; doing so literally, as for example, when he calls Peter Satan because he wants to prevent him from suffering, and metaphorically when he speaks of the baptism he has to receive which already constrains him and of the chalice (of God's wrath) which he must drink. Jesus also says much more, calling his death a "lytron," a ransom (Mk. 10:45) and this for "the many," meaning surely not Israel alone but an unlimited number of persons. The same idea recurs in the words of Eucharistic institu-

tion. Attempts to edit these words away are futile; indeed,
were it possible to do so, then the entire faith of the
Church in the Eucharist, the Last Supper and the associated presence of Christ would be destroyed.

But we can say still more. Both the synoptics and John
show Jesus living in the light of a mysterious, approaching
"hour." This is the hour which, in Luke, he "earnestly
desires..." and which began with the Last Supper (Lk.
22:15); the hour which filled him with fear and yet could in
no way be avoided: "Now is my soul troubled. And what
shall I say? 'Father, save me from this hour'? No, for this
purpose I have come to this hour. Father, glorify thy name"
(Jn. 12:27f.).

When, then, would Jesus first have known of the hour
awaiting him? The answer is, from the very beginning.
Not only is this the teaching of the Fathers of the Church
who vie with each other in repeating that Jesus was born
ultimately in order to be able to die and to die precisely this
redemptive death, but the whole style of Jesus' life is itself
also a revelation of this: the way he expresses himself in
words that he can only venture to use if he knows beforehand they have his passion as their pledge; the way he
announces in advance the Father's forgiveness and himself
forgives sins in the name of God, something only possible
because he already draws in anticipation on the reconciliation between God and the world which the cross will
effect; the way he heals souls and bodies by miracles which
are, as it were, loans from the atoning passion. He knows
he will have to repay in the future all he has so lavishly
dispensed. In no sense whatever did the passion come upon
him from without simply because he was so unlucky as to
rile the Jewish and Roman authorities, which would not
have happened had Scribes, Pharisees and Sadducees only
got to know him better. Nor is it permissible to say that
Jesus provoked his own death. In no way did he himself
seek it, as is clear from the occasions when, by flight or

concealment, he eluded his would-be murderers for the very reason that his hour had not yet come.

But there is an objection. As Israel's Messiah it was his mission, surely, to bring the people back to God, and he did his utmost to carry out this task as witness, so effectively, the tears he shed over an obdurate Jerusalem: "How often would I have gathered your children together...and you would not" (Mt. 23:37; Lk. 19:41). But would he really have expended all this toilsome zeal if he had known beforehand that he was to fail? The answer is Yes; an unqualified Yes. And the proof lies in the vocations of the great prophets: Isaiah, Jeremiah, Ezekiel. From the very beginning, from the moment of their calling, they are told that all their labor will be in vain and yet they tackle their mission with all their strength and even with hope. This is a point that to my knowledge, exegetes largely neglect.

But we must seek to delve still further into Jesus' consciousness. The Son of God came to teach us what attitudes should replace the self-will and disobedience of Adam in our relationship to God: obedience to absolute good and to love, obedience out of love, obedience to death on the cross, meaning for him the hour of darkness and the chalice full of God's wrath at the sins of the world. It is because of this obedience that we are reconciled to God. Obedience is better than sacrifice, it says in the Old Testament. It is also better than independence and personal knowledge. The Son's obedience was of far greater value than what, in their reverence, the Fathers and Scholastics sought to attribute to Jesus, namely the perpetual beatific vision of the Father, plus a thorough knowledge of all earthly things and in particular of his own destiny. But how could such a person, knowing more about everything than any other man and able to settle anything on the basis of his own plenitude of insight, have desired to expose himself from moment to moment to the inspirations of the Holy Spirit in order to do continually not his own but his Father's will?

Jesus has exactly that knowledge which is necessary for
his mission as Israel's Messiah and God's Servant; that is,
as the world's Redeemer. This means, first, consciousness
of a Messianic mission to Israel; he is to lead the chosen
people to conversion and to the original understanding of
God's covenant and law. Hence his every step involves
total dedication and the ever living hope that this step will
prosper: "zeal for thy house consumes me." We perceive
this in Jesus' every discourse, every miracle, every absolution from sin. Secondly, it means the knowledge that,
despite every earthly frustration God's plan of salvation
will finally be accomplished by him; after the judgment
which will be enacted in the "hour of darkness," on the
"day of Yahweh," comes the great atonement of which
every prophet down to God's servant himself had spoken;
his own appalling mission to reconcile the world to God
would, despite everything, succeed because of the bearing
of the unthinkable burden of the sin of the world by the
Lamb of God. After all he is from his baptism the beloved
Servant and the Son, with whom God is wholly well-
pleased and to whom, for that reason, the whole salvific
will of the Father is entrusted. But thirdly, it meant a
definite lack of knowledge of the hour: "Of that day or
hour no one knows, not even the angels in heaven, nor the
Son, but only the Father" (Mk. 13:32). This is vitally important and is to be taken absolutely literally. Jesus knows that
the hour is steadily, inexorably approaching: "My hour has
not yet come"; but he leaves it entirely in the Father's
hands. He does not strive to neutralize the pain of the
coming encounter. He follows his own advice: "Do not be
anxious about tomorrow, for tomorrow will be anxious for
itself. Let the day's own trouble be sufficient for the day"
(Mt. 6:34). Albeit God's only Son, he is at the same time the
first Christian, the exemplar for all his followers.

He knows neither more nor less than is needed to
accomplish his universal, once-for-all, redemptive mission.

He has unshakable faith that the Father will lead him through every darkness until his mission is accomplished, unshakable hope in the God of Israel who is the God of all peoples, infinite love, accepting in adoration every disposition of the Father, even the ultimate forsaking and the terrible thirst—for the absent God.

But, surely God's Son is himself God and as such omniscient. Indeed. But that is not the same as saying that he wanted to pass on his divine attributes altogether to his human nature. At this point we are faced undoubtedly with mysteries we shall never fully penetrate. But we can say one thing: just as the Son as God from all eternity receives the fullness of divinity and therefore complete omniscience from the Father, so, in gratitude and no less eternally, he gives back himself and all he has to the Father, holding it at the latter's exclusive disposal. On such a basis we can at least partly understand how, when the Son's eternal procession from the Father assumes the form of mission to the world, he can leave his divine attributes with his Father in heaven, without losing them. Indeed, that is to say, though he was in the form of God, he emptied himself (Phil. 2:7) precisely in order to be able, as a man, to be obedient unto death. God's eternal Trinitarian life is obviously enough of a life to allow this. Sacred Scripture explicitly declares as well as constantly presupposes that one who is truly God is able at the same time to become truly man. For Christian theology, no other portrayal of Jesus Christ can qualify as faithful.

4. Jesus Christ and the Foundation of the Church

It has become the custom to cast doubt on the idea that Christ founded the Church. The principal reason given is that he seems to have expected an imminent end to the world apparently envisaging no break between the destruction of Jerusalem and that of the world. No one, of course, has a mind to contest his foreseeing the destruc-

tion of the city; after all such second-sight is a common,
obviously natural phenomenon, and, more ad rem, the
prophets themselves made similar, highly detailed predictions of the same event. Inevitably one thinks of Isaiah; he
foresaw that Jerusalem would be destroyed root and
branch and yet the inconceivable would happen, out of the
apparently dead stump that remained, a new shoot would
spring, the royal shoot intended by God from the very
beginning and called by the prophets the "holy remnant."

Yet Jesus says that not only Jerusalem but the whole
world is about to end. Here even Catholic exegetes find
themselves in a dilemma. But let us look at things as Jesus
looked at them. He has to reconcile with God not just past
and present humanity but all mankind. In a real way then
he bears the guilt of the generations still to come, and with
his cross he literally achieves this to the very end of the
world. It is only when our world comes to an end that the
resurrection, as such, has its full consequences, however
much or little chronological time may be left for others. It
is definitively, eschatologically true for him to say to his
disciples: "Be of good cheer, I have overcome the world"
(Jn. 16:33). "When Christ had offered for all time a single
sacrifice for sins, he sat down at the right hand of God,
then to wait until his enemies should be made a stool for
his feet" (Heb. 10:12f.), that is, until his eschatological
act has had its effect upon what remains of subsequent
history. He could, without any difficulty, realize that, for
him, the world was at an end even though for others
historical time would continue. Hence his remark: "Truly, I
say to you, there are some standing here who will not taste
death before they see the Son of man coming in his kingdom" (Mt. 16:28), or as Mark has it: "before they see the
kingdom of God come with power" (Mk. 9:1). As we said in
the first section, the Risen One, having accomplished his
mission, is in truth the kingdom.

This brings us to a highly controverted area: the visions

that the disciples had of Jesus after his resurrection. The whole of Christianity depends upon their being true. To make illusions or hallucinations of them would be to sunder the Church from the historical Jesus. We cannot here treat in detail of what invalidates the rationalist and liberal attempts to abolish the Easter event. Briefly, though, it is the change wrought in the disciples by their repeated experience. Their whole world was turned upside down; doubt became certainty and timidity the courage to witness. But the strongest of all arguments for the Easter event is Paul's experience on the road to Damascus. How could an hallucination have caused the instantaneous conversion of this rabid persecutor of Christians and turn his whole life around by 180 degrees? And so Paul, in the oldest New Testament text we possess, aligns the appearance to him with those to Peter and the Ten. Only in light of the Easter appearances could the obvious meaning of the life, teaching, miracles, and above all, the Passion of the earthly Jesus, dawn on the disciples; now that the last syllable of the Word had been uttered the whole made the beginning intelligible.

A fearsome hurricane had swept through the spirits of the disciples and naturally it took time for the turbulance to settle. Jesus' work, complete in itself, still had to be carried on by them. They had both to go beyond the covenant with Abraham and Moses and yet to keep to it even as it was being consummated. The future now opening before them, be it short or long, confers a final meaning on what has been begun in Jesus' life. Month after month, year after year, they experience ever more intensely the saying that "when the Holy Spirit of truth comes he will guide you into all the truth; for he will not speak on his own authority, but...take what is mine and declare it to you" (Jn 16:13-14). By this they understand that it is not the Holy Spirit who in the first place establishes continuity between Jesus and the Church; they themselves have already been chosen by Jesus and sent out to preach and heal; they have already renounced everything for his sake. Exegetes may make what they like of Jesus' words: "Do this in memory of me," but on the basis not just of the Last Supper but also of the bread broken with them by the Risen One, the apostles themselves realize that Jesus' gestures are to be continued and are not less important or less relevant for the ages to come than for the present. And after Easter too the full significance of the power given them to forgive sins on earth, and so in heaven, comes home to them. When they preach they will not have simply to refer back to the unique act of atonement on the cross, but they will be able to actualize that atonement in specific personal acts of absolution or, if need be, of retention until such time as the sins can be authentically forgiven. Paul's Letters and the Acts of the Apostles provide us with eloquent examples of this.

For the rest, matters take their course quite naturally. There are no consultations or disputes about whether the disciples of Jesus retain the powers previously given them, whether Peter should still have a primacy within the apostolic college or whether the apostles can delegate their powers to others—Paul, for example, as the Letters to the Corinthians show, does this so much as a matter of course that we need hardly be surprised to see the apostles later, just as unquestioningly, handing on the powers necessary for church leadership to their successors, who in their turn would hand them on, no less unquestioningly, as we learn in the Letter to Titus: "This is why I left you in Crete, that you might amend what was defective and appoint elders in every town as I directed you" (Ti. 1:5).

The whole mysterious structure of the Church, even though unique vis-à-vis every other earthly kind of community, evolves without any problem. No one will contest either the pastoral authority established by Jesus himself —"he who hears you hears me"—nor the common fellowship among all: "one heart and one soul," "you have one teacher and you are all brethren" (Mt. 23:8). And the Church, ever incomparable, takes her stand in realms both visible and invisible: visible in her preaching, sacraments, authority, and creed, but at the truest level of her life, as of the Christian's, invisible: "your life is hid with Christ in God" (Col. 3:3). The Church and her members draw their life from Christ in his completeness, from his earthly existence, his death, his resurrection, and so live at once in the here and now and in that beyond opened to them because they have died with Christ. Being rooted in eternal life the Church and the faithful have the power to work here below in accordance with the demands of their mission. They are as much heavenly as earthly. They sympathize with the lot of the world. These paradoxes of the Christian life were there from the start, fixed and unchallenged, and there has been no need, as the millennia have passed, for any essential alterations. From this point of view the Church is an instance of spontaneous generation, not unlike one of the macro-mutations of evolution, and at the same time, it is evident that her whole distinctive essence originates in the existence of the pre-resurrection Jesus, as that of the butterfly in the caterpillar.

To develop, the Church did not need Jesus to provide it with involved charters of foundation or detailed instructions. To take its origin from him, it sufficed to have his example, his choice and teaching of the disciples, and the promise of the Holy Spirit to guide the disciples into all the truth and action they could not yet understand. All the foundations were laid in Jesus, yet it was God's Spirit who built up the Church upon those foundations. Both facts are obvious. As Jesus himself said: "One sows and another reaps. He who reaps gathers fruit for eternal life, so that sower and reaper may rejoice together" (Jn. 4:36-37).

Translated from the German by Hugh Gilbert, OSB of Pluscarden Abbey, Scotland.

CHRISTOLOGY FROM ABOVE
AND CHRISTOLOGY FROM BELOW

Louis Bouyer, CO

*(Priest-theologian
from France)*

In the past few years, much has been made, in theological circles, of a distinction between what has been called "Christology from above" and "Christology from below." The traditional Christology of the Church, inherited from the councils of the first centuries, is what one has come to characterize as "Christology from above," insofar as it starts, it is said, from the presupposition that Christ is fundamentally a divine being, having only assumed and made his own our humanity, not without transforming it in the process: "the Son of God made man," it is argued, being necessarily seen as a man the like of whom no man has ever been or ever will be.

Such a presentation, it is added, could easily be accepted as long as men were ready to believe in any kind of mythology. However, nowadays, with the general acceptance of the scientific view of the world, to think or to talk of Christ in such a way has become not only unacceptable, but more or less meaningless. What we need, therefore, is a "Christology from below," i.e., a Christology starting from the indisputable fact that Christ was a man, a complete man: indeed the fullest possible exhibition of what a man could be, should be. Thus and thus only could he be accepted by modern men as having made real for us in a supreme way what God is for us, and especially in what sense he made of Christ and wants to make of all of us through him, *the* Son of God par excellence, true sons of God also without, for that, having to be as it were dehumanized, but rather made in the end, in spite of all our failures, what man was intended to be from the first by God our Maker.

Now, such being the context of the apposition, what are we to think of it? Is the so-called "Christology from above" to be discarded altogether, or, at the least, to be put on the shelf for the time being? Is the "Christology from below" the only one that can make sense for modern man?

To put the matter as simply as possible I would say that Christology from below has ever existed, but it has been always (and will certainly remain forever) the Christology (or any of the Christologies) either of people fumbling to express their feeling that Jesus was unique but not succeeding to hit upon his uniqueness, or of people not any longer able to grasp and retain what is implied in that uniqueness.

We see that with the disciples answering his question: "What are people saying that I am?" they will say: "Some say that you are John the Baptist, others that you are Jeremiah or another of the Prophets..." and maybe it was so natural at first to say such things (as, for some, it still remains), though with an inner feeling that they could not believe, that this explains why Peter himself, in the speeches quoted by the *Acts*, will be able still to talk of him as of "a man approved by God and passing through the world doing good," while already being categorical that "no other name has been given to men through which they can be saved...."

However, when the first disciples themselves are pressed by Jesus: "But *you*, what are you saying of me?" it springs forth impulsively: "You are *the* Son of God!" And already, conscious of the fact or not, we have moved from all the possible Christologies from below to a Christology from above, which will have to make clearer its affirmations, but never go beyond what has been said already, as at a point of no return.

In fact, we see here the threshold of what is properly

explicit faith, in Jesus as the Savior of mankind. As long as it is not reached, we can draw near what will be Christianity, but it is only when this line has been past that we are in it indeed. And, we must add immediately: whatever may be the good intentions of Christians who want or seem to fall back again from Christology from above to Christology from below, when they are realizing what they are doing or wanting to do, they must acknowledge that they despair of Christianity as it has ever been, and will ever remain, if it is ever to subsist.

Are we then to accept the idea that Christianity has become impossible for modern man, insofar as it would imply a mythological view of Christ, dehumanizing him?

Now this is just a double mistake, involving first, a mistaken view of what was mythology at the time when the gospel took shape, and, second, of what is really of lasting value in the modern feeling of what a man should be to be truly man indeed.

On the first point, it must be said that what can be described as mythological accuracy is precisely what is now suggested to us as a modern substitute for the traditional Christian view. Nothing, in fact, was more characteristic of the mythologies contemporary of the beginning of the Christian era than that shallow view of divinity which enabled men to "divinize," in speech, at least, all kinds of outstanding personalities, while it was agreed that they were and remained, in spite of that, just of the common sort of men, including not only limitations, but vices of all kinds. For it could be said of the "gods" of the mythologies that they were greater than the average man no less in their capacity for evil than in their capacity for good!

A mythological god was just a monstrous man...as would be that exalted man, and nothing else, that our Christologies from below want to make again of Jesus. That which all Christians worthy of the name have always acknowledged in Christ, is, in opposition to that, not that merely aggrandized human nature that any Christology from below can suggest, but that human nature finding an unheard of perfection in being indubitably assumed into the absolute transcendence of the biblical God; that, precisely, which the sole humanity of Christ in appearing to be his own and exclusive possession has come to reveal in its fullness.

Conversely, the fear that such a Christology from above, which clearly is not a creation of the councils but the spontaneous growth into adequate words of what the disciples came to believe and testify, as soon as they were fully aware of what it was that was so unique in their Master, should involve some evaporation of his manhood, as they knew it, is completely baseless. Their faith, the faith of the Church, it should never be forgotten, is the faith of men who believe, first of all, that God, as the creator of mankind, has willed it "after his own image." To fear that the "image," therefore, would be ruined, or distorted in any way, by acquiring an unheard of community, or rather communion, with its Model, is sheer nonsense.

Finally, what is to be feared of a Christology from above, as though it were in danger of dehumanizing Christ, is not that it should be too faithful to its principle, but rather that it might be lacking in consistency with it. Such is the case of all forms of Arianism, of Monophysism, and no less of Nestorianism. But it is precisely to safeguard the primitive, the only genuine Christology from above of the gospels that the councils have produced their definitions.

CHRISTOLOGY AND CREATION

Luc Richard, OMI
*(Weston School of Theology,
Cambridge, Massachusetts)*

The world is charged with the grandeur of God.
It will flame out, like shining from shook foil;
It gathers to a greatness, like the ooze of oil
Crushed. Why do men then not reck his rod?
Generations have trod, have trod, have trod;
And all is seared with trade; bleared, smeared with toil;
    the soil
Is bare now, nor can foot feel, being shod.

And for all this nature is never spent;
There lives the dearest freshness deep down things;
And though the last lights off the black West went
Oh, morning, at the brown brink eastward, springs—
Because the Holy Ghost over the bent
World broods with warm breast and with ah! bright
    wings.

Gerard Manley Hopkins
God's Grandeur

Hopkins' poetic sense reflects the incredible God-given goodness of Creation. No matter what we humans have done and can do, Creation still holds the heart of things in freshness not in a mechanistic way but "because of the Holy Spirit." Creation is a grace, God's very first grace, a lasting grace.

Yet our theological tradition has witnessed the separation of nature from grace. This is the inevitable result of a theology in which Creation has been separated from Incarnation and Redemption. The disadvantage of this polarization is evident not only in the obvious degradation of nature as over against grace, but also in the juxtaposition of reason and faith, of works and faith, of evangelization and development, of religion and politics. All these dichotomies are indicative that certain elements of Creation are autonomous, i.e., outside the realm of grace and the personal will of God—and must therefore either be without value or else brought by force to subjection to God. There is a tendency to either banish grace into the inner life and therefore simply accept the political, economic status quo, or to force one's own Christian understanding upon the political and economic structure.

A certain ambiguity is already present in the New Testament about these separations. Paul writes in Phil. 3:30: "Our homeland is in heaven," and in Col. 3:1f.: "If then you have been been raised with Christ, seek the things that are above, where Christ is seated at the right hand of God. Set your mind on things that are above, not on things that are on earth." The same can be heard in other parts of the New Testament. "Here we have no lasting city, but we seek the city which is to come" (Heb. 13:14). We find in the New Testament two different understandings of the meaning of the word "world." [1] The first meaning is the world as God's creation (Acts 17:24) the totality of all that is created (Jn. 1:10; 1 Cor. 3:22). To affirm that the world is created is a profession of faith: God is the ruler and Lord of all. Yet the New Testament does not affirm unambiguously the Lordship of God over all creation. The final rule of God over the world is always perceived eschatologically. Since God's lordship and sovereignty is not without ambiguity, the New Testament presents us with another meaning of the word "world"—the world as *Kosmos*, as fallen Creation. This fallen world is in longing for a future and different world.

In Jewish thought there is a temporal conception of a coming world, a world which is better than the present; yet the Kingdom of God is experienced as operative in this world; this rule of God is perceived in hope and expectation for a change for Israel. As E. Schillebeeckx writes:

> The more radically this world deviates from God's creative ordinance and contradicts it, the less talk about the kingdom of God is talk about this world, because this world as people experience it is simply not "in order." In that case, the kingdom of God increasingly becomes something which is not experienced in this world. Only in this way does the kingdom of God appear as an *alternative* to this world, an alternative the reality of which will only be revealed in the last days. This gave rise to the apocalyptic world of two levels, where everything that was to take place among men had been prepared for from eternity in a heavenly world.[2]

Notwithstanding the experience of a world where God's rule is not fully realized, Israel remains faithful to its understanding of God as Creator and Conservator. In this perspective one must seek a deeper grasp of the apparent New Testament dualism and its rejection of this world. While the world is created good by God (Jn. 1:10) yet there is a need for salvation and illumination. The world is obscured by the sin of men/women—yet it is also the object of God's mercy and love. As John writes, "God so loved the world. . ."(3:16). Jesus himself is named "the savior of the world" (Jn. 4:42). Some of the Kingdom of God can be realized on earth. In the humanity of Jesus Christ that Kingdom has appeared and made itself present. Despite the difference between this world and the Kingdom of God we are not bound to a two-story universe. While the final consummation of the Kingdom, of the life of grace, is in the future, yet it is now present in this world.

A salvation history that would have nothing to do with a Creation history would be without meaning. God, the transcendent world-maker, is the agent and author of both processes. As the world-maker, God is the Lord of all—the moon and the stars, the beasts on earth and humankind are all his subjects. In a Christian context that unity of history and salvation history cannot be perceived without perceiving the intrinsic connection between God the Creator and Jesus Christ the Redeemer. This connection can be understood in a variety of ways. The early Christians identified Jesus the Christ in some way with the world-Creator. Jesus as Christ was seen as the divine agent, God's instrument in the world-Creation.[3] The New Testament claims that Jesus was the divine Word (Jn. 1:1ff.) by whose power and authority the world was created and constituted. Christ is the beginning of the creation (Col. 1:15) but at the same time, he is heir to everything there is (Heb. 1:2) in that all things were created, through him and for him (Col. 1:15).

The basic problematic with this approach has been apparent over the centuries. Can Christ be both Creator and created? The identification of Creator with Christ has often led to a Christocentric understanding of God and a separation of Creation from Redemption. What is needed is to approach the relation between Creation and Incarnation from another perspective. Belief in God the Creator has to become the source of belief in the gracious and forgiving God who has revealed himself in the human person of Jesus. As we read in Heb. 11:6, "Whoever would draw near to God must believe that he exists and that he rewards those who seek him." God is Creator both of everything that exists and also of salvation. The person of Jesus must be seen as a creation of God-Jesus, the person in whom the task of creation has been successfully accomplished. The Incarnation must be perceived as "intensified Creation," as the "fulfillment of Creation." Jesus in this understanding is perceived as the summit of the general relation of creature to Creator.

To understand in what way Jesus is the revelation of the Creator in his own humanness, and how the Incarnation is intensified Creation, one must look at the Old Testament background.[4] Israel's belief in Creation arose out of her experience of God within history, and is shaped by this experience. The understanding of God as Creator of the world follows from the experience of God as Creator of Israel. The Exodus, the Covenant, the Settlement provided the models for the understanding of God as Creator of the world.

It is from the experience of the Exodus that Israel's idea of total dependence on Yahweh emerges. "Has any god ever attempted to go and take a nation for himself from the midst of another nation, by trials, by signs, by wonders, and by war, by a mighty hand and an outstretched arm, and by great terrors, according to all that the Lord your God did for you in Egypt before your eyes?" (Dt. 4:34).

The almighty God shaped Israel in the same way a potter shapes a statue out of clay. But this shaping of Israel is not simply done once and for all. There is an ongoing process. God establishes a creative covenant with Israel. "The Lord spoke to you out of the midst of the fire . . . . He declared to you his covenant" (Dt. 14:12-13). Creation and covenant are totally out of God's freedom. Yet there is a demand for a response on the part of Israel, a response that implies obedience, faith, trust, worship.

The creation of the world through God's Word brings about all reality under the Lordship of God. All that is, is in a relation of obedience to God. The dependent status of creatures is evident in the idea of existence as obedience to a God-given command: "The heavens are thine, the earth also is thine; the world and all that is in it, thou hast founded them. Know that the Lord is God! It is he that made us, and we are his" (Ps. 100:3). Under the formal aspect of being creatures, all men/women are equal: "The rich and the poor meet together; the Lord is the maker of them all" (Prv. 22:3). Coming from God, Creation is essentially good. "And God saw everything that he had made, and behold, it was very good. Everything created by God is good, and nothing is to be rejected if it is received with thanksgiving; for then it is consecrated by the word of God and prayer" (Gn. 1:31; 1 Tm. 4:4-5). Creation is therefore a gift. Creation as such then is covenantal emerging from a faithful and free God. As God's free act, Creation is revelatory and requires on the part of man/woman praise and thanksgiving. "Sing to the Lord, bless his name; tell of his salvation from day to day. Declare his glory among the nations, his marvelous works among all the peoples! For great is the Lord, and greatly to be praised; he is to be feared above all gods. For all the gods of the peoples are idols; but the Lord made the heavens" (Ps. 96:2-5).

In the Old Testament, God the Creator does not exist in a relation of competition to Creation. God is in constant and faithful relation to Creation, giving guidance and life in human history. God undergoes an "Exodus" from himself. Even the revelation of Yahweh's name "I am" (Ex. 3:14), while pointing to God's transcendence, implies a real presence—"I am with you" (Ex. 3:12).

While God as Creator is almighty and brings about reality by the power of his Word, yet since this Word is a personal Word it has authority over Creation in a dialogical manner. It is a word of invitation, of promise of radical demand, yet in need of response. God's authority in the act of creating is in need of the acknowledgment of Creation itself. This aspect has been stressed by Emil Brunner:

> Because in the full sense God can be Lord only of such a subject who in free personal decision acknowledges Him as Lord, He wills this independence of the creation.... He wills to be their Lord because only in His being known as Lord is He really Lord in the complete sense.[5]

Because God creates in a personal way, and not as an abstract power, what God has created must stand in a relationship to him. As Claus Westerman writes:

> The text is making a statement about an action of God who decides to create man in his image. The meaning must come

from the Creation event. What God has decided to create must stand in a relationship to him. The creation of man in God's image is directed to something happening between God and man. The Creator created a creature that corresponds to him, to whom he can speak, and who can hear him—God created man in his image, corresponding to him, so that something can happen between God and the creature—is presented here in narrative form: the possibility of something happening between God and man consists in this, that God gives man a command and man can only relate himself to this in freedom. He can abide by what has been commanded or he can reject it. In both cases he sets himself in either a positive or negative relationship to him who commands. The freedom of this relationship arises only from the command; without the command there would be no freedom. [6]

To accept God as Creator is to profess to accept God as one's Lord; it is to accept one's dependence upon God. It is to accept one's existence as gift, in gratitude; it is to accept God as the faithful one. There can be no acceptance of Creation and of Creator without self involvement. [7] Knowledge of God through Creation demands not simply a form of contemplation but an active doing; it involves a righteous man/woman. As B. Gartner writes:

> In the Old Testament, knowledge of God, worship and ethics are fused, and become one expression of the God-fearing man's acknowledgment of the One God. [8]

As D. Evans writes, "Ignorance of God is an active ignoring of him, a refusal to know him—that is, a refusal to be loyal to him, to obey him, to glorify him, etc."[9]

The Old Testament understanding of Creation is presented as an organizing concept; it does not simply state something about a situation—it affirms that whatever is, is related to an originating principle. Such an understanding of Creation does not simply present itself to our mind for an intellectual acceptance. It implies a conversion on our part, a metanoia. Augustine marked the turning point of his journey when he grasped fully the fact of Creation:

> ...considered all things that are of a lower order than your-self, and I say that they have not absolute being in themselves, nor are they entirely without being. They are real insofar as they have their being from you.[10]

Creation because of its manifold and personal dimension both on the part of God and the fact of creatures is best expressed in a story, in a parable. The language of parable, as many have expressed in a variety of ways, is self-involving.[11] Creation in the Old Testament, Kingdom of God in the Old Testament, are interpretative parables. To accept a parable is to adopt an attitude, one by which one lives so as to be in rapport with God and thus be enabled to understand the parable better. The parable functions as event of revelation only when the bearer enters the new world of the parable.

In summing up the Old Testament doctrine on Creation, one can say that for the Old Testament everything is understood as having been created by God; that God the Creator can be trusted for he is the reliable one; that Creation is the fundamental ground for a reflected depend-ence, trust, thankfulness, and obedience to God (Is. 17:2; 22:11; 40:26ff.; Ps. 103:32; 119:73).

In the Old Testament, Creation becomes the ongoing trust that God will intervene redemptively in our lives: "Yet thou, O Lord, art our Father; we are the clay and thou art our potter; we are all the work of thy hand. Be not exceedingly angry, O Lord, and remember not iniquity forever. Behold, consider, we are all thy people" (Is. 64:8f.), and "Yahweh, God of Israel...thou hast made heaven and earth. Incline thine ear, Yahweh, and hear...save us, we beseech thee, from his hand [the hand of the enemy], that all the kingdoms of the earth may know that thou, O Lord, art God alone" (2 Kgs. 19:15f., 19). And, lastly, Creation in the Old Testament must be seen as the presupposition for and as the foundation of a fruitful relationship to God, that of prayer, worship, obedience, and trust.

The Old Testament in a variety of places has affirmed that God created out of love, out of his own free will (Ps. 102:26-28; 103:19). Yet there remains the question whether Creation is also the full and definitive expression of the Hesed of God, of his ongoing, merciful love of man/woman, always ready to forgive. For God, to create is also to save. The creative power of God is almighty and irresistible and brings reality to existence—"O house of Israel, can I not do with you as this potter has done, says Yahweh. Behold, like the clay in the potter's hand, so are you in my hand" (Jer. 18:6). God as Creator is a God of life and not destruction (Ps. 135:6-9). God has shown himself to be father in Creation; the same father who has saved Israel from bondage and given them the land. In the "Song of Moses" (Dt. 32:1-43) we find the passionate dimension of God's fatherhood as Creator: ". . . is this how you repay the Lord, you brutish and stupid people? Is he not the father who formed (qana) you? Did he not make you and establish you?" By being called Father, God is honored as the Creator: "Is not he your father, who created you, who made you and established you?" (Dt. 32:6). "Have we not all one father? has not one God created us?" (Mal. 2:10). In the Old Testament, God's fatherhood is related not only to his care for Israel but also for his care as Creator for all that there is. Israel appeals to God as Father in the light of their experience of him as Creator who determines their lives in every aspect.

The New Testament says that what has happened and what happens between God and man/woman has its center in what is regarded as Jesus of Nazareth. In Creation, man/woman is given the ability to relate to God as Creator freely. The New Testament in turn says that this took place in a radical way in the person of Jesus Christ. Jesus

Christ is the parable of the God-Creator-Creation relationship. There is no abnegation of God's creative power in the Incarnation but a deeper expression of it. At the beginning of his book on the parables, C. H. Dodd writes:

> There is a reason for this realism of the parables of Jesus. It arises from a conviction that there is no mere analogy, but an inward affinity, between the natural order and the spiritual order; or as we might put it in the language of the parables themselves, the Kingdom of God is intrinsically like the processes of nature and of the daily life of men. Jesus therefore did not feel the need of making up artificial illustrations for the truths he wanted to teach. He found them ready-made by the maker of man and nature. That human life, including the religious life, is a part of nature is distinctly stated in the well-known passage beginning "Consider the fowls of the air..." (Mt. 6:26-30; Lk. 12:24-28).
>
> Since nature and supernature are one order, you can take any part of that order and find in it illumination for other parts. Thus the falling of the rain is a religious thing, for it is God who makes the rain to fall on the just and the unjust... and the love of God is present in the natural affection of a father for his scapegrace son. This sense of the divineness of the natural order is the major premise of all the parables.[12]

Jesus Christ in himself is the prime parable of what radical creatureliness is. In Jesus is expressed and realized the fullness of what it means to be created and who the Creator is. The universality of Jesus' meaning must be discovered in the manner of his being a creature, in his acceptance of creatureliness and of God as Creator. In the person of Jesus Christ, Creation and Redemption take human form and are given to us in a parabolic and revealing way. As Paul writes in 2 Cor. 5:17: "If anyone is in Christ, he is a new creature."

This parabolic revelation is the nature of Jesus' life, ministry, death, and Resurrection. Jesus' life is marked by his relating to God as *Abba*. As R. Hammerton-Kelly writes: "Abba means that God is love: it is a representation of the primordial experience of reality as good, expressed three thousand years before Christ in the hymn to the Moon god, Sin from Ur—'Compassionate and merciful Father in whose hand the life of the whole land lies.' "[13] The heart of Jesus' message is the universal Fatherhood of God as symbolized in the Kingdom of God. Jesus places the Father Image and reality of the Kingdom of God at the center of his doctrine of God. Throughout the Gospel and in the words and gestures of Jesus, his own trust in and loyalty to the encompassing and universal love of God is made evident. In Lk. 12:30-31, Jesus underlines the fact that there is no need for anxiety because God's rule is benevolent. One can trust God since God is really Father, Abba. The Kingdom of God is the role of God, Creator-Father. The coming of the Kingdom is in the realization of salvation.[14] For the completion of the Kingdom means the fulfillment of all human yearnings and the end to human suffering.

As Isaiah describes it: "On this mountain the Lord of hosts will provide for all peoples a feast of rich food and choice wines, juicy, rich food and pure, choice wines. On this mountain he will destroy the veil that veils all peoples, the web that is woven over all nations; He will destroy death forever. The Lord God will wipe away the tears from all faces" (Is. 25:6-8). As Pannenberg writes: "The Kingdom of God, according to the Old Testament, is expected in the form of establishing love and justice in the society of man."[15] The Israelites could trust in God for it is he who

> secures justice for the oppressed, gives food to the hungry. The Lord sets captives free; the Lord gives sight to the blind. The Lord raises up those that were bowed down; the Lord loves the just. The Lord protects strangers; the fatherless and the widow he sustains, but the way of the wicked he thwarts. The Lord shall reign forever; your God, O Zion, through all generations. Alleluia (Ps. 146:7-10).

For Jesus, the Kingdom of God is the doing of God's will for all Creation, Creation being brought to wholeness and completion in the living of its covenanted relationship to God. In his book, *On Being a Christian,* Hans Küng has a useful summary of Jesus' understanding of the Kingdom:

> It will be a kingdom where, in accordance with Jesus' prayer, God's name is truly hallowed, his will is done on earth, men will have everything in abundance, all sin will be forgiven and all evil overcome.
>
> It will be a kingdom where, in accordance with Jesus' promises, the poor, the hungry, those who weep and those who are downtrodden will finally come into their own; where pain, suffering and death will have an end.
>
> It will be a kingdom that cannot be described, but only made known in metaphors: as the new covenant, the seed springing up, the ripe harvest, the great banquet, the royal feast.
>
> It will therefore be a kingdom—wholly as the prophets foretold—of absolute righteousness, of unsurpassable freedom, of dauntless love, of universal reconciliation, of everlasting peace. In this sense therefore it will be the time of salvation, of fulfillment of consummation, of God's presence: the absolute future.[16]

In the person of Jesus is embodied the Kingdom of God and in his understanding of his relationship to God as Father is given to us a parable about Creation and Creator. In the person of Jesus, in his life, ministry, death, and Resurrection, we have the revelation of Creator and Creation, of the right relationship between Creator and Creation. Jesus was perceived by the early Church as the fulfillment of Scripture because he was the fulfillment of mankind-in-relation-to-God. Jesus embodied the true Adam, a renewed humankind. At Jesus all the lines of God's relations with men/women are found to be meeting. What Israel was meant to be in relation to God, Israel had failed to be; but Jesus had succeeded. According to C. F. D. Moule: "Israel represented the position intended in the Genesis creation stories and in Psalm 8, for Adam: mankind, obedient to God. What had been found in the Christian experience of Jesus Christ far transcended the parochialism of Israel; it was the fulfillment of man."[17] Jesus is perceived as the second Adam. Jesus as second Adam is understood as gathering into himself the destiny of all Israel and so of all mankind. In Paul's Letter to the Romans where Adam typology is most evident, salvation is understood as the reversal of Adam's fall; it is the reshaping of man/woman into the image of God. Salvation is the restoration of man/woman to that image in which Adam had been created. Now, for Paul, Jesus is the indispensable model or pattern for this process. As J. D. G. Dunn writes:

> For it is not Adam, unfallen Adam, who is the image into which believers must be transformed, but Christ: it is God's purpose to conform believers "to the image of his Son" (Rom. 8:29); "as we have borne the image of the man of dust, we shall also bear (phoresomen) the image of the man of heaven" (1 Cor. 15:49); it is Christ who is the "image of God" (2 Cor. 4:4; Col. 1:15; cf. 3:10).[18]

In his total life, ministry, death, Jesus' life is marked by these New Adam characteristics. As Dunn writes: "Christ's earthly life was an embodiment of grace from beginning to end, of giving away in contrast to the selfish grasping of Adam's sin, that every choice of any consequence made by Christ was the antithesis of Adam's. . . . "[19]

This "Original Adam" characteristic is expressed in a variety of ways in Jesus' life and ministry. Jesus' experience of prayer is clearly one such expression.[20] Jesus has a radical orientation to the Father. His prayer reveals that Jesus lived entirely from the Father. Jesus blessed food (Mt. 14:19; 15:36; 26:26) and attends the Sabbath service (Lk. 4:11). As William M. Thompson writes:

> According to the synoptics, Jesus' entire life is embraced in an atmosphere of prayer; that is, in a posture of openness to the

Father. Jesus' public ministry begins and ends with prayer (Lk. 3:21, 23:46). When he chooses the twelve (Lk. 6:12f.), in teaching (Lk. 11:1), before curing (Mk. 9:29), and while trying to strengthen his disciples (Lk. 22:32), he prays. Particularly at critical moments, as at the Garden of Olives, does he pray (Mt. 11:25; Lk. 10:21; Mk. 14:35-36). Further, he prays in the Aramaic vernacular (Mk. 14:36; 15:34), removing prayer from the sacral liturgical sphere where only Hebrew was spoken, expressing its everyday quality. In Jeremiah's words, Jesus places prayer "right in the midst of everyday life." Finally, his relationship to the Father in prayer is grounded upon the relational God of pathos, as the uncommon address "Abba" reveals. This Aramaic colloquialism, taken from the child's language of intimacy, reveals the depth of Jesus' relationship with his Father.[21]

Jesus' prayer reveals that Jesus lived entirely from the Father, something that has been expressed by another pervasive characteristic of Jesus: his obedience (Mk. 14:36; Lk. 2:49; Phil. 2:8; Rom. 5:19; Heb. 5:7-9; Jn. 5:19; 5:30). Jesus' obedience acknowledges God to be Creator and man to be creature. Obedience is the sign of regained creaturehood, of regained humanity. Paul designates Jesus as the obedient one, because by his death he restores man to the righteousness of true obedience—an obedience that acknowledges God to be Creator and man to be creature, a creature who renounces all pious and rebellious attempts at self-salvation. For in Paul, obedience is the sign of a humanity reestablished in the proper order. For Paul, Jesus' life and death are expressions of his obedience.

As the "Original Adam," Jesus reveals himself as the authentic believer, "the pioneer and perfector of our faith" (Heb. 12:2). According to W. Thüsing:

> Jesus should be understood not simply in the manner of an example, but rather as the one who lived this faith in a unique way and whose faith has now attained permanence, with the result that he now gives his own power to believe in this way.[22]

There is on the part of Jesus an unconditional trust in God's power and readiness to help. On the Cross Jesus expresses this radical faith and trust: "Father, into your hands I commend my spirit" (Lk. 23:46).

The grounds of Jesus' gift of self on the Cross and the reason for his Resurrection is this faith and trust in God the Father-Creator. Jesus' letting-go is anchored in his trust in God's benevolence. Jesus' kenosis in faith is rewarded by exaltation. As W. Thüsing writes: "In the New Testament the risen Jesus is still regarded as really man. ... He is seen as the one who was open to the absolute mystery and as the one who received from the absolute mystery what he had to hand on to others."[23] In Rom. 6:10, Paul affirms of the risen Jesus that he "lives for God." There is a permanence of this life from God and for God that crosses into the realm of eternal life and exaltation.

Prayer, obedience, faith and trust in God-Father-Creator are the characteristics of Jesus' life. They are the expression of the radical acceptance of creatureliness—of the fundamental structure of his relation to God. Jesus is the one who sees himself and the whole of his life in the context of receiving and giving. Receiving is the fundamental expression of his being. And yet in that acceptance of radical creatureliness, Jesus is most authentically human. In Jesus we have the affirmation that the more deeply one's own creatureliness is accepted, the more one discovers oneself, the more radically one is made free for one's possibilities. In Jesus we have the unique culmination of the general Creator-Creation relationship. In his personal unity with God, Jesus is the fulfillment of the human destiny. Human destiny is to have its origin permanently in God, to be permanently grounded in absolute mystery; to be radically different and yet one with God. Being from God and being totally dependent upon God in no way cancels out human personhood, individuality or independence. The deepest self of man is constituted by its relationship with God. This is directly related to man/woman's capacity for the infinite. The actualization of that capacity through God's graciousness constitutes the deepest dimension of a person's self-being. The more a creature participates in God's being, the more the creature is someone itself. As Karl Rahner writes about Jesus Christ:

> Hence we can verify here, in the most radical and specifically unique way the axiom of all relationship between God and creature, namely that the closeness and the distance, the submissiveness and the independence of the creature do not grow but in like proportion. Thus Christ is most radically man, and his humanity is the freest and most independent, not in spite of, but because of being taken up, by being constituted as the self-utterance of God.[24]

Man/woman is never so truly and fully personal and autonomous as when he/she is living in complete dependence on God. The more complete our dependence upon God is, the more radical is our human autonomy. As Michael Buckley writes:

> Dependence upon God is not like dependence upon another thing in the universe. God is not another being in the universe; God is source. One could argue that dependence upon another being, something with which we exist, can sometimes take away human autonomy. Whatever be the truth of this, whatever be the judgment of its validity after any number of critical distinctions, it is radically false when applied to human dependence upon God. For genuine reality is not threatened by the ground of all reality; on the contrary, reality is established in its freedom and autonomy by its ground. The dependence upon God is that which establishes my reality, not what denies it. We are infinitely different from God—with the absolute difference that creation has brought about—and we never merge amorphously with God. The created does not merge with the uncreated. Creation is the

guarantee of our autonomy. Our autonomy is precisely the effect of the action of God.[25]

What we have in the person of Jesus as the Christ is intensified Creation. In Jesus Christ the dimension of creatureliness is not eliminated but sharpened. As J. B. Metz writes: "The human nature of Christ is not 'lessened' by being taken up into the divine Logos, made simply into a dead tool, a mere accessory, a gesture of God within the world, but given its hitherto unsuspected full, human authenticity: Jesus Christ was fully man, indeed, more human than any of us."[26] Being "accepted" by God is a freeing act since it is fundamentally a kenotic act. Again Metz writes: "God's divinity consists in the fact that he does not remove the difference between himself and what is other, but rather accepts the other *precisely as different from himself.*"[27] To be accepted by God is to be set free to be oneself. Christ is the chief exemplification of God's gracious giving of himself and the actualization of man's own response. In Jesus we have the unique culmination of Creation's own response. In Jesus we have the unique culmination of the general creator-creation relationship. Incarnation becomes, then, a characteristic of God's being with us. Incarnation as applied to Jesus is a specific case of what is true about God's presence. Incarnation expresses something decisive about God's self-communication to his total Creation.

That I believe in God the Creator implies that I believe in God's love without limits, without condition, that I believe in a God of involvement, of relationship, that in creating, God from being rich has made himself poor, that the activity of God in Creation is precarious. In my belief in Creation, I bear witness to the revelation in Jesus Christ that God's innermost being is one of love for humankind and for human deliverance. Christology becomes a specific way of making belief in Creation more precise. Christology is concentrated Creation. In Jesus Christ, God reveals himself as the one who takes the side of Humanity, without condition. The "human cause" becomes God's cause, irrevocably. As David Tracy writes:

> In response to the Christ event as God's own self-manifestation the believer dares to trust: to trust in the God who is Love, now re-presented new in the Christ event; to trust in the gift and command to the self to trust and live in freedom and in love; to trust in the ordinary and its extraordinariness; to trust in history and its struggle for justice, for authentic freedom, for the coming reign of love, for the future as God's own future enabling and commanding us to enter into that struggle in the present; to trust in nature and its manifestations and its yearnings for the whole; to trust in Jesus Christ as primal word and sacrament of God's own self.
>
> In the moment of re-cognition enabled by the event of representation, the Christian believer senses that here in the event of Jesus Christ the primal word and manifestation of God and thereby of ourselves, of history, nature, the whole is decisively revealed as an event not of our own making yet confirming our deepest longings for wholeness in the whole.[28]

NOTES

[1]Cf. Hermann Sasse, "Kosmos," in *Theological Dictionary of the New Testament*, G. Kittel, ed., Vol. III, pp. 867-899.

[2]E. Schillebeeckx, *Christ: The Experience of Jesus as Lord*, (New York: Seabury Press, 1980) p. 554.

[3]Cf. D. von Allmen, "Reconciliation du monde et christologie cosmique," RHPR 48 (1968), pp. 32-45.

M. J. Suggs, *Wisdom, Christology and Law in Matthew's Gospel*, (Cambridge, MA, 1970).

J. G. Gibbs, *Creation and Redemption: A Study in Pauline Theology*, (Leiden, 1971).

J. Murphy-O'Connor, "I Cor. 8:6: Cosmology or Soteriology?" RB 85 (1978), 253-267.

[4]Cf. G. von Rad, *Genesis: A Commentary*, tr. J. H. Marks, (London, 1961).

Claus Westermann, *Creation*, tr. John S. Scullion, S.J., (London, S.P.C.K., 1974).

H. Renckens, *Israel's Concept of the Beginning: The Theology of Genesis*

1-3, tr. C. Napier, (New York: Herder and Herder, 1964).

   B. Anderson, *Creation versus Chaos: The Re-interpretation of Mythical Symbolism in the Bible* (New York, 1967).

   [5]E. Brunner, *The Divine-Human Encounter*, (London, 1949), P, 40, p. 45.

   [6]C. Westermann, *op. cit.*, p. 56.

   [7]Cf. Donald Evans, *The Logic of Self-Involvement*, (New York: Herder and Herder, 1969).

   [8]B. Gärtner, *The Areopagus Speech and Natural Revelation*, tr. C. H. King, (Uppsala, 1955), p. 116.

   [9]D. Evans, *op. cit.*, 197-198.

   [10]*Confessions of Saint Augustine*, tr. R. S. Pine-Coffin, (Baltimore, 1961), VII, 11, (147); cf. also VII, 20, (154); X, 6 (212).

   [11]Cf. J. Dominic Crossan, *Language, Hermeneutic and the World of God*, (New York: Harper & Row, 1966).

   [12]C. H. Dodd, *The Parables of the Kingdom*, (London, 1935), p. 2.

   [13]R. Hammerton-Kelly, *God the Father*, (Philadelphia: Fortress Press, 1979), p. 81.

   [14]Cf. W. Pannenberg, *Theology and the Kingdom of God*, (Philadelphia: Westminster Press, 1969).

   Norman Perrin, *Jesus and the Language of the Kingdom*, (Philadelphia: Fortress Press, 1976).

   Rudolph Schnackenburg, *God's Rule and Kingdom*, (New York: Herder and Herder, 1963).

   [15]W. Pannenberg, *op. cit.*, p. 79.

   [16]Hans Küng, *On Being a Christian*, (Garden City: Doubleday, 1976), p. 215.

   [17]C. F. D. Moule, *The Origin of Christology*, (Cambridge: Cambridge University Press, 1977), p. 152.

   [18]Cf. James D. G. Dunn, *Christology in the Making*, (Philadelphia: Westminster Press, 1980), pp. 98-128.

   [19]*Ibid.*, p. 106.

   [20]*Ibid.*, p. 121.

   [21]William M. Thompson, *Jesus: Lord and Savior*, (New York: Paulist Press, 1980), p. 171.

   [22]W. Thüsing, *A New Christology*, (New York: Seabury Press, 1980), p. 144.

   [23]W. Thüsing, *op. cit.*, p. 92.

   [24]K. Rahner, "On the Theology of the Incarnation," *Theological Investigations*, Vol. 4, (1974), p. 117.

   [25]Michael J. Buckley, "Within the Holy Mystery," in *A World of Grace*, ed. Leo O. Donovan, S.J., (New York: Seabury Press, 1980), pp. 46-47.

   [26]J. B. Metz, *Theology of the World*, (New York: Herder and Herder, 1969), p. 26.

[27]*Ibid.*

[28]David Tracy, *The Analogical Imagination,* (New York: Crossroad, 1981), p. 336.

THE FULLNESS OF CHRIST'S SACRIFICE

Colman E. O'Neill, OP

(*University of Fribourg, Switzerland*)

The new covenant in my blood

The historical approach to the New Testament has made valuable contributions towards our understanding of the significance for faith of Christ's suffering and death. This has involved the painstaking reconstruction of what must have been Jesus' own state of mind as his ministry led him into an ever more threatening situation of conflict with the authorities and of disbelief on the part of the people which, at the end, could have only one outcome. While there is not universal agreement among exegetes either as to the historicity or as to the interpretation of many of the passion-sayings attributed by the gospels to Jesus during the course of his ministry, there is no dispute worthy of note as to the authenticity of the central sayings attributed to Jesus at the Last Supper at the breaking of the bread and the sharing of the wine-cup. It is likewise accepted that with these words Jesus was giving his own interpretation of his approaching death.

The careful analyses that have been made of these eucharistic words provide one of the major aids given by contemporary biblical exegesis to both Christology and sacramentology. What emerges most clearly from the context of a paschal meal, from the interwoven themes of the Suffering Servant of Isaiah 53, the covenant and the eschatological Kingdom, and from the cultic symbolism of both actions and words, is that, for Jesus, his death was to be understood as a sacrifice offered "for many for the forgiveness of sins" (Mt. 26:28). Even more significantly, it was to be understood as marking the inauguration of the "new alliance" (so, explicitly, Lk. 22:20 and 1 Cor. 11:25, with a direct allusion to Jer. 31:31).

It would be hard to exaggerate the importance for systematic theology of these biblical orientations. There is, on the one hand, the intensely human and heroic theme of the Servant, the "man of sorrows" who "carried our sorrows," who "bore the sin of many" and on whom, indeed, the Lord has laid the "iniquity of us all" (Is. 53). On the other hand there is the mysterious reference of this whole human drama of willing involvement in the suffering of others to the initiative of God. God is said, by an affirmation of faith, to be intervening in this way in order to establish among men his definitive sovereignty. This is the new covenant spoken of in Jeremiah: "I will put my law within them, and I will write it on their hearts...for I will forgive their iniquity, and I will remember their sin no more" (Jer. 31:33-34).

By the combination of these two aspects, the human and the divine, the notion of sacrifice, as applied to the death of Christ, is transformed in such a way that theologians need to use the greatest delicacy in their treatment of it. Analogies drawn from the history of religion can be of only minor relevance; even those drawn from the cultic practices of the Old Testament can have only a relative value. Then it still remains for the systematic theologian to formulate in a coherent way and by reference to his own hermeneutic principles the significance that the New Testament accounts have for the life of the Church today.

In the New Testament itself, Hebrews already grapples at length with the problem of reinterpreting, in the light of the event of Christ, the categories elaborated in connection with the Jewish sacrifice of the Day of Atonement. Strikingly, in view of the allusion in the words of institution of the Eucharist, appeal is made to Jeremiah 31:31-34, the latter being understood as a description of the merciful forgiveness on the part of God which marks the new covenant (Heb. 8:1—10:8). Interiorization of the divine law, which according to the prophet is the gift of God's mercy, is taken to be the distinctive mark of Christ's priestly sacrifice: " 'I have come to do thy will, O God,' as it is written of me in the roll of the book" (cf. *ibid.*, 10:5ff.). It is in terms of this obedience but also of the certitude that Christ has risen ("for Christ has entered...into heaven itself...in the presence of God on our behalf," *ibid.*, 9:24), that the analogy of the Jewish ritual is applied to Christ.

The thought-structures thus drawn from the Jewish liturgy are apt to seem remote and artificial today. It is to St. Paul that we must turn to find, expressed in a few words, the radical newness of the sacrifice of the new covenant: "All this is from God, who through Christ reconciled us to himself and gave us the ministry of reconciliation: that is, God was in Christ reconciling the world to himself"(2 Cor. 5:18-19). Colossians puts it in similar fashion: "For in him all the fullness of God was pleased to dwell, and through him to reconcile to himself all things ...making peace by the blood of his Cross" (Col. 1:19-20).

What makes Christ's sacrifice unique and what achieves it as sacrifice is the fact that it is God who takes the initiative, it is his merciful forgiveness that breaks through the otherwise insoluble dilemma of sin. And yet this in no way takes away from the total human dedication of Christ to the will of the Father and to the holiness of God. This apparent paradox of the Scriptures is what the systematic theologian must attempt to resolve. To make any progress he must appeal to the nature of the fundamental relations that exist between created liberty and God. The initiative in the sacrifice is both divine and human. The two are taken up into a harmony that is certainly mysterious since the divine action is involved. Equally certain there is nothing to be gained by dark references to a "reconciliation of opposites," for this kind of paradox refers to nothing beyond the subtle game that idealists play, with their own mental constructs for pieces, on the board of their own minds. In the real existence of Jesus it was his own liberty, his own suffering and his own death that were at stake. To say that in this human drama God is personally and objectively active is to appeal to the mystery of divine transcendence which reveals itself in its most astonishing form in created liberty.

The harmony that unites Christ's total self-sacrifice and the saving will of the Father is deeper even than the love that certainly inspired Christ's every action; it is, in the final analysis, the harmony of created being and freedom with its divine source. Little wonder, then, that the Christian community, conscious of the sinfulness of all men except this one, of the universality of evil, should come to see that God himself, the creative Word, was the subject of Christ's human activity, for only so could the self-destroying image of God be restored. Yet, though this new beginning was necessary, the harmony that was reestablished in the activity of the incarnate Word is not, in itself, something that is within the possibilities only of the divine Son. When the Spirit is sent, every man is "open to God" (*capax Dei*; cf. St. Thomas, *Summa theol.*, I, q. 93, a. 3 ad 3: *capax summi boni*), capable, that is, of entering in supreme liberty into union with the Creator and even, because it is the divine Spirit who is sent, into that vision where the Trinity will be known as it is (cf. 1 Jn. 3:2).

Christian intuition, as expressed by St. Paul in particular, grasps, with awe yet with no hesitation, that, in the case of Christ, it is no contradiction to attribute salvation both to the human events of Christ's life and death and at the same time to the intervention of God who alone can forgive sin. This same intuition goes further and can grasp, perhaps only fleetingly and obscurely, how, as a consequence, the life of the Christian can, also without contradiction, be said to be the life of Christ himself (cf. Gal. 2:20) since faith in him establishes union with the act of salvation which is his. He sends the Spirit, the gift of God, but "where the Spirit of the Lord is, there is freedom" (2 Cor. 3:17). The freedom of which St. Paul speaks, though he frequently relates it to freedom from the Law, is in fact much more radical. Freedom from external prescriptions is only a consequence of the new covenant in which, because God takes the initiative, human freedom itself is liberated so that it recognizes as its own interior law the will of God.

"For you": exegesis and presuppositions

It may seem that rather more has been drawn out of the simple words, "blood of the new covenant," than the text itself warrants. In fact, what has been done is to apply to the text a general hermeneutic; and, since God is spoken of in the text, such a hermeneutic is necessarily ontological. A return to the text should help to determine whether the resulting systematization is legitimate.

The words of institution, in the context of the Passover meal, were richly symbolic, filled with resonances of history and its prophetic interpretation. At the Last Supper this verbal symbolism was taken up and developed in the whole ritual, even though it was the words themselves that most clearly departed from the traditional usages. After the blessings of the bread and the cup came the invitations to take, eat and drink. St. Mark underlines the fact: "and they all drank of it" (14:23); while St. Paul adverts specifically to the renewal of the memorial ritual in the Eucharist: "As often as you eat this bread and drink the cup, you proclaim the Lord's death until he comes" (1 Cor. 11:26). Jesus was not content to give a theoretical interpretation of his approaching passion and a verbal promise of the coming Kingdom. The very setting required it: the disciples were already drawn into the mystery of his death and resurrection, though they can have barely understood this at the time. Their eating and drinking made them sharers in the blessings that were to flow from this new covenant being established by God with the world. So much was this so that, in spite of the menacing symbolism of the blood being poured out, there was already an evocation of the new wine they would drink together when the Kingdom would finally have come.

This far-ranging complex of word and symbol is brought to a point when Jesus indicates that what is about to happen to him is to have the significance of a sacrifice offered by him "for you," "for many," or, as St. John seems to suggest, "for the life of the world" (cf. Jn. 6:51c). There is much discussion among exegetes as to the precise meaning of "for" in this context (*huper*; in Matthew: *peri*) and principally as to whether it stands for "in place of" or "in favor of" or something else. Clearly, the nuance attached to the preposition is not to be decided by philology. Whatever translation is adopted already depends on a developed theology concerning the saving significance of Christ's sacrifice. At this point exegesis is determined less by references to Old Testament sacrificial vocabulary, which by the nature of the case is inadequate to express the newness of the Christian mystery, than by presuppositions which are not necessarily scriptural at all.

The various readings of the present text afford, in fact, one of the most striking examples of how much the individual exegete's presuppositions establish his theological hermeneutic. There is necessarily called into play, perhaps only implicitly or even without the interpreter's adverting to the fact, an appeal to some form of systematic theology current in a particular Christian tradition. The project of making the Scripture its own interpreter, understood as a total hermeneutic, has never been more than an abstract theory; and, though an appeal to the present guidance of the Holy Spirit provides a satisfactory way of breaking the hermeneutic circle, it can be of no help to the community if it is made simply in virtue of individual experience.

So, for example, the notion of "vicarious sacrifice" or the

whole series of variations on the theme of "representative or substitutionary satisfaction or atonement" most frequently offered as readings of Christ's "for you" are patently systematic concepts. They can be read from the text only because the reader takes it for granted, on other grounds, that he will find them there. The examples given appear most naturally in the work of exegetes belonging to the Reformed traditions. They derive, however, from late-medieval nominalistic theology with its speculations on the "absolute power" of God. If, indeed, the will of God is assumed to be an arbitrary force, in no way immanent in the values of the created world, then it is quite logical to conclude that it can substitute any created thing for any other—and why not the sufferings of Christ in place of the punishment due to the sin of the world? It is a salutary reaction when this sort of speculation is rejected as a deformation of man's own ethical values; less so, however, when a purely humanistic interpretation of the mystery of Christ's mediation is offered in its place, for then one rationalism replaces another.

There is little reason to suppose that the post-medieval Catholic tradition dealt with the matter in a more satisfactory way. Though its sacramentalism inclines it towards a non-idealistic, and so non-pantheistic, stress on the immanence of God, its theologians have not been unaffected by nominalistic theories of redemption. The rationalistic tendencies which may be found in St. Anselm's theory of "satisfaction," at least when it is isolated from its author's presuppositions, have proved hard to escape from. In the Catholic tradition this shows itself in a whole body of speculation on the "merits," "satisfaction," and "sacrifice" of Christ. This conceptualizes Christ's mediation, possibly as a result of the polemic of the Counter-reform, in a way that may fairly be described as legalistic; it is certainly very far from Christian personalism. Once again reaction sets in; and Catholic versions of political or

"critical" theology are just as much given to ethical reduc-
tionism or barely concealed political theory as are those of
non-Catholics.

"Objective" redemption and the problem of liberty

The hypothesis is here put forward that the root of the
problem summed up in the "for you" lies in an uncritical
acceptance of the common distinction between "objective"
and "subjective" redemption (the metaphor of the New
Testament being deliberately retained). At this point it
does not matter whether a given theologian accords real
value to the notion of "objective" redemption or whether
he thinks it to be simply a mythical remnant which needs to
be systematically eliminated from Christian thought. In
either case it is assumed that the notion of "objective"
redemption and its real distinction from "subjective"
redemption are an adequate, if schematic, representation
of traditional understanding of what Christ is believed to
signify for the world. Those who do, in fact, accept this
scheme of thought may not always be conscious of how
foreign its presuppositions are to those who seek to formulate an anthropology worthy of the name, one that takes
human freedom seriously. It is, in any case, difficult for
anyone who attempts to explain what is meant by "objective" redemption to avoid falling back on the themes of
"merit" and "satisfaction" which, in the case of Christ, will
be described as "capital," belonging to the head. This is
clearly metaphorical language. When it is used to attribute
a supra-personal ethical value to the works of Christ, it is
hard to see how it can be reconciled with the ethical
responsibility of those who accept his mediation.

Both Catholic and Protestant traditions were drawn to
the concept of "objective" redemption by such terms as
ephápax, the "once for all" of Hebrews: "By that will [of God]
we have been sanctified through the offering of the body
of Jesus Christ once for all" (10:10; cf. 7:27; 9:12; with 9:26

and 1 Pt. 3:18). Here there is, quite evidently, something that must be taken into account in any valid theory of redemption. It is, however, quite another thing to assume that a phrase used to underline the uniqueness of Christ's role in salvation is properly understood as a simple expression of the irrevocability that characterizes any person's past action. Naturally, few theologians would let it go at that; appeal would certainly be made to the complementary notion of *plèroma,* fullness, and cognate terms (Jn. 1:16; Rom. 15:29; Eph. 1:10, 23; 3:19; 4:13; Col. 1:19; 2:9; etc.) and indeed to the whole Pauline concept of the "mystery" (esp. Eph. 1 and Col. 1). The difficulty is that these are all categories which carry marked symbolic overtones and which, for that reason, lend themselves to a variety of systematic interpretations.

The point that needs to be made is that non-biblical presuppositions will inevitably be called into play in the interpretation of redemption, even if the interpreter is willing to permit his most cherished ideas to be placed in question by the text. In particular, the idea of "objective" redemption, when it is used in such a way that the person of Christ is isolated, even only conceptually and provisionally, from his members, from those who, in one way or another, actually receive salvation, appears to be one of the most widespread of such non-biblical presuppositions. In its most ill-considered form it develops into a theory of substitutionary punishment; but the basic non-personalistic assumption is not radically altered so long as any trace of juridical thinking remains hidden in the account given of salvation in Christ.

If Christians are to learn from the challenge of humanistic thinking which equates their belief in Christ with a renunciation of human responsibility, they must re-think in personalistic terms the tradition they have received. The first step, and the most decisive, involves overcoming the dichotomy between "objective" and "subjective" redemption. Purely conceptual distinctions must be transcended and a synthesis sought in the reality of whatever it is that Christ did "for us" and the reality of our own liberty. A synthesis itself is, evidently, conceptual in structure; but it should reflect as much as possible the lived experience of faith in Christ and of the dialectic of actual Christian liberty.

The question is, of course, what basis can be used for such an effort of reflection. To call on the tradition of infant baptism is, perhaps, to make a significant point; but it does little to clarify the problem of adult freedom. It will not do either simply to have recourse to the "signs of the times" so as to discover the challenges which Christian liberty must face. Christian practice is certainly the only test that can be applied to discover the authenticity of belief; and practice is ineffective if it is not relevant to the social and political situation in which a local community finds itself. But this leaves unresolved the question of what is specific about Christian involvement; and so it leaves unresolved the further question of whether, and in the name of what, the Christian should be critical of the "signs of the times." Nor will it do simply to reproach the practical theologies with failure to elaborate a prior theory of Christian practice; this seems remote from reality and, perhaps, more a justification for university theology than an existential approach to the Christian life.

A Eucharistic hermeneutic

Within the Catholic tradition there would appear to be a possibility of combining a theoretical statement about the personalism of Christian redemption with a nontheoretical way of living which would reflect that personalism and at the same time give it direction in its confrontation with contemporary issues. It is not being suggested that this would replace the normal functioning of conscience; it would, however, place moral decision within a specifically

Christological context. The possibility being spoken of is to be discovered in the Catholic tradition's understanding of the Eucharist as sacrifice.

This may, at first sight, appear to be an unduly controversial approach to the Eucharist. Most ecumenical discussions prefer to establish agreement on the Eucharist as communion before turning to the disputed question of sacrifice. This may tell as much about uncertainty on the Catholic side as to why its tradition maintains the symbol of sacrifice as it does about possible misconceptions about the matter on the non-Catholic side. Whether or not such misgivings are justified must depend on the results given by using the hypothesis here being suggested.

The account of the Last Supper indicates that the disciples who ate and drank thereby shared in the sacrifice of Christ. When the biblical symbolism is set within the non-biblical framework established by the distinction between "objective" and "subjective" redemption, the interpretation that spontaneously suggests itself is that eating and drinking communicate to believers the "fruits" of Christ's sacrifice. Given the systematic presuppositions, the equally systematic conclusion is quite natural. And since it at least formulates clearly the dependence of the believer on Christ's mediation, there is no reason to dispute what it claims, even if the terminology is thought to be unfortunate. It is still legitimate to raise the question whether the conceptual framework does not limit the scope of the conclusion so that the latter presents only a partial truth.

This question can be raised in virtue of the need for developing an adequate hermeneutic of the biblical text. The claim here being put forward is that a Catholic hermeneutic not only may, but must, appeal to the community's authentic understanding and experience of the Eucharist in order to grasp the full implications of the Supper narratives. This is patently the case with regard to the meaning

of the words, "This is my body" and "This is my blood."
As written, they could mean all sorts of things, as those
exegetes who adopt a purely historical approach amply
testify. But within the Catholic tradition they must mean
at least one thing, that this *is* his body and *is* his blood,
however theologians manage to cope with such affirmations of faith. It is also the case with regard to the meaning
of "eating" and "drinking," that is, to the way in which
believers are called to share in the sacrifice of Christ. The
Catholic tradition's insistence on the sacrificial character
of the Eucharist, however its details are to be accounted for
in systematic theology, points to a belief that sharing in the
so-called "fruits" of Christ's sacrifice involves sharing also
in the personal offering of himself that made Christ's
sacrifice what it was and what it is in the Mass. With this
reading in view it does not seem by chance that St. Mark,
who alone notes that "they all drank of" the cup (14:23),
insists more than St. Matthew on the implications of the
readiness of the sons of Zebedee to drink the cup that Jesus
must drink: "The cup that I drink you will drink; and with
the baptism with which I am baptized, you will be baptized"
(10:38; cf. Mt. 20:23).

There is, however, a further step to be taken in the
application of this Eucharistic hermeneutic. If the Eucharist entails the personal willingness of those who share in it
to enter into the personal offering of Christ, this dimension of Christian experience must modify the conceptual
framework of our understanding of Calvary itself. So far
from being in any way vicarious or involving the substitu-
tion of another's suffering for our own, it assumes its full
dimensions only when those who believe in Christ ratify it
by relating to it, in faith, their own existence and all that it
involves. St. Paul, very conscious of his own special mission to the Gentiles, did not hesitate about relating his own
experiences in this way to Christ's sacrifice: "In my flesh I
complete what is lacking to Christ's afflictions for the sake

of his body, that is, the church" (Col. 1:24). Once this startling proposal has been made, there is no reason why it should be limited to those who preach the word. It undoubtedly places in question any clear-cut distinction between "objective" and "subjective" redemption. Christ's saving action is not to be isolated from his members' personal involvement in it. The "for us" of the Supper and of Calvary takes on its full significance and achieves its existential realism only when it becomes "in us," that is, when Christians join with Christ in personal self-offering; and this can be done only in freedom.

There is some justification for theologians' having spoken of "objective" redemption. The reference is to the earthly mysteries of Christ (and sometimes to his resurrection also) and to their saving significance as belonging to the unique Mediator. A Eucharistic herme-neutic, however, shows that this is an abstract view of redemption. In the first place, the Eucharist necessarily places emphasis on the present action of the risen Christ (cf. Heb. 7:23ff.). His priestly, sacrificial service is fulfilled only when, and as, the redeemed join in his offering of himself to the Father and to mankind. It is towards this end that the Eucharist, through the presence of the risen Christ, is sacrificial. Secondly, and more fundamentally, the Eucharist places in proper perspective the whole ques-tion of the use of sacrificial terminology with reference to the Christian mystery. It restores the primacy in sacrifice to the intervention of God who alone can forgive sins; and this is shown in the Eucharist to be the basis of whatever is called sacrifice in the Christian dispensation.

In the symbolic structure of the Eucharist it is, doubt-less, the dimension of communion that most clearly alludes to this divine initiative. The dimension of sacrifice, how-ever, places the emphasis on the most profound truth of all: that the forgiveness of God is an act of his love; and that his love, unlike human love or the forgiveness that expresses it, is a *creative* love, in the fullest sense of that word. Here, once again, is the mystery of the new covenant. Its creativity bears its first fruits in the humanity of Christ. Through him, for he is the head, this divine creative love is at work in those who are united to him. This is finally why Christ can never be isolated from his members, nor "objective" from "subjective" redemption. Redemption is a work of divine love, calling up sacrifice in the person of Christ only in order that it might be created as well in the hearts of all who accept this mystery.

Theological categories for redemption

When sacrifice, understood as human response to God's creative act of mercy, is made the central category for thinking about the Christian mystery, other, more restricted, categories adopted by the Christian tradition can be given their due importance. "Merit" and what it signifies lose any remnant of commercial connotation and take on the meaning of Christ's response to the Father's love, which makes possible the response of others as Christ sends the Spirit into the world. Christ's "satisfaction" and the suffering which that word conceals are no longer in any way suspect of being a penalty exacted for sin by an inscrutable divinity. It is rather that, in the person of Christ, the divine creative love is brought to all men in no other way than in the conditions created by sin. This divine initiative and this pain that was borne in history become redemptive and "satisfactory" in truly existential terms only when, through the love that comes through Christ, others learn to find in suffering and in the alleviation of suffering a way towards God that inevitably begins in a situation created by sin.

The Eucharist as a lived experience, one that gives direction to the whole Christian life, provides the only proof that Christian logic can know: the sufferings of Christ become redemptive when the gift of divine love, the Spirit sent by Christ, allows and requires that others willingly share in them. It is in this Christological and Eucharistic context that the term "spiritual sacrifice" of Christians (cf. 1 Pt. 2:4-10; Rom. 12:1-2; Heb. 13:11-16) becomes more than a metaphor for ethical endeavor and takes on all its realism in the economy of salvation.

There are, in fact, no categories, not even those taken from the highest tradition of the Jewish people, that are adequate to express the newness and the universal significance of Christ, the Messiah who is believed to have come. Where such categories as are available are useful is in reference to the humanity of Christ, to his obedience, his dedication to the holiness of God, his love for the Father and for all men, all of which led him to his death. They may be applied as well, due proportion being guarded, to all those actions of Christians which share, in their own measure, in the moral rectitude of Christ. Indeed, those that relate directly to personal involvement in sin—most pertinently "satisfaction"—are applied more properly to Christians than to Christ. But all categories reveal their incapacity to grasp the mystery when the attempt is made to take into account the fact that God's mercy, combined with his respect for the dignity even of sinful man, acts through the human actions of Christ. It is because Christ sends the Spirit that those who thereby belong to him are able to share in his moral rectitude, to offer his sacrifice because they offer themselves, to make true satisfaction by overcoming sin in themselves and in society. It is the gift of the Spirit that raises all this out of the sphere of simple moral emulation and into the mystery of the union between Christ and those who receive from him the Spirit.

St. Paul has an intuition of the mystery, but he cannot really find the words for it. He can afford glimpses, as when he says, excusing his past anger: "The love of Christ controls us, because we are convinced that one has died for all; therefore all have died. And he died for all, that those

who live might live no longer for themselves but for him
who for their sake died and was raised" (2 Cor. 5:14-15).
Here there is an attempt to transcend the ordinary categories but it is threatened by incoherence. The sacrifice of
Christ encompasses both his death and his resurrection;
the personalities of Christ and Christians first merge ("all
have died") and then separate as the moral responsibility of
the latter comes to the fore; and, most striking of all,
Christ's "for all" is transposed into the Christians' "for
him." The Letter to the Colossians will seek for a higher
reconciliation of the crumbling categories, precisely by an
appeal to the divinity of Christ: "He is the image of the
invisible God, the first-born of all creation; for in him all
things were created...through him and for him. He is
before all things, and in him all things hold together. He is
the head...the beginning, the first-born from the dead
...that in everything he might be preeminent. For in him
all the fullness of God was pleased to dwell, and through
him to reconcile to himself all things" (1:15-20). It is
because it is the divine Word of creation who is active in
Christ, who is indeed the subject of his action, that his life,
death and resurrection can be the first restoration of the
true liberty of the image of God in an otherwise sinful
humanity. It is likewise because it is the divine Word who is
the subject that Christ's liberty may become, through the
Spirit, the personal liberty of all those who are created in
the image of the Trinity.

St. Paul can say the same thing in terms of the Eucharist,
and in a context which is specifically sacrificial, for the
sacrament crystallizes the mystery: "The cup of blessing
which we bless, is it not a participation in the blood of
Christ? The bread which we break, is it not a participation
in the body of Christ? Because there is one bread, we who
are many are one body, for we all partake of the one bread"
(1 Cor. 10:16-17). St. Augustine clearly grasps the dynamic
sense that is to be attached to the metaphor of the body

when it is associated with the sacramental body of Christ. It is common knowledge, he says, for those who truly take part in the Eucharist that "the Church herself is offered in the offering which she presents to God" (*The City of God,* X, 6). This is where the fullness of the sacrifice is achieved.

Bibliography

R. Cessario, O.P., *Christian Satisfaction in Aquinas. Towards a Personalist Understanding,* University Press of America, Washington, DC, 1982.
C. E. O'Neill, O.P., *Sacramental Realism. A General Theory of the Sacraments,* Michael Glazier, Inc., Wilmington, DE, 1983.

A CHRISTOLOGICAL PARAENESIS
Philippians 2:5-11

Stanley B. Marrow, SJ
*(Weston School of Theology,
Cambridge, Massachusetts)*

The spate of twentieth-century contributions to the Philippians "hymn" gives no indication of subsiding. From Johannes Weiss' first recognition of the poetic genre of Philippians 2:5-11[1] in 1899 down to its most recent structural analysis by Ambrogio Spreafico in 1980,[2] the analyses, insights, and interpretations have maintained a steady flow. Thus, any added contribution, however modest in aim and limited in scope, must seem foolhardy; and if foolhardiness be subsumed—as a defect—under the capital virtue of Prudence, then the author of the present remarks has to confess his imprudence and plead both as an excuse and a justification nothing other than that hunger and thirst for "hearing the word of the Lord" which Amos (8:11) proclaimed and which impels—or ought to impel—all the study of sacred Scripture. If there be a claim to anything new in these remarks, it is not so much the insight attained or the interpretation proposed, but rather the very modest one of juxtaposing the structural evidence with the theological exegesis.

In the more recent contributions to the study of the Philippians hymn that followed R. P. Martin's valuable *Carmen Christi*,[3] the articles of J. Carmignac (1971/72),[4] Pierre Grelot (1973),[5] Morna D. Hooker (1975),[6] Jerome Murphy-O'Connor (1976),[7] and Ambrogio Spreafico (1980)[8]—have, I believe, given a significantly different turn to the course of interpretations and made it possible to question certain assumptions about the genre of the pericope (whether it is a hymn, and how it is structured), its theological exegesis (whether it outlines a two- or a three-stage Christology), and its intended meaning within the immediate context of the epistle.

I. A. The Genre of the Pericope

"It is a singular fact," remarks R. P. Martin, "that it was not until the beginning of the twentieth century that the unusual literary character of Philippians 2:5-11 was detected and classified."[9] This very fact itself ought to give the reader pause. Its singularity, of course, means that John Chrysostom, Theodoret, Theodore of Mopsuestia and other patristic commentators, whose knowledge and mastery of Greek was more native than acquired, had missed the obvious. This is not impossible; but, given the considerable stature of these commentators, rather unlikely. Perhaps what they missed was simply not there. Highly rhetorical, poetic and even *hiératique*[10] though it be, the pericope of Philippians 2:5-11 is still not poetry—not Greek poetry in any case; and Greek is the only text we actually possess. To be sure, no one can deny the rhetorical devices evident in the composition, the stylistic balance and parallelism, the rhythmic cadence and what Cerfaux calls the studied *agencement des périodes;*[11] but all these argue to a highly elaborate prose, even a poetic prose, but do not, in and of themselves, constitute Greek poetry.

The expedient of retroverting the present Greek text into a putative Aramaic original is just that, an expedient. Apart from the fact that rendering a translation back into its conjectural original is a tricky and unsure business at best, the arguments for and against such a pre-Pauline Aramaic original are by no means settled.[12] Nevertheless, the temptation to divide the hymn into strophes, cola, hemistichs and chiasmus has been too strong to resist ever since E. Lohmeyer set his hand to it in *Kyrios Jesus* (1928).[13] Even a recent study by M. D. Hooker, who clearly admits that, "If this passage is poetry, it is certainly not Greek poetry," succumbs to the temptation of "reconstruction" in poetic form of Philippians 2:6-11.[14]

But if the Greek patristic commentators failed to notice the "poetry," it is simply because Philippians 2:6-11 is not a poem or an ode; and its structural components, in their evident symmetry and parallelism, would yield surer results in exegesis if they were analyzed as they stand in the Greek text and not as they might be reconstructed into some suppositious Aramaic *Urtext*. If modern commentators find the temptation to restructure or to retranslate difficult to resist, the real difficulty lies not so much with the rules of prosody as with the presupposed stages of the Christology. For the moment it is sufficient to say that if we refer to the pericope of Philippians 2:5-11 as a "hymn" then we ought to do so with the understanding that the term so used is used loosely, the way one might speak of 1 Corinthians 13 as a hymn.

I. B. The Structure of the Pericope

There is no denying the fact that the hymn in Philippians 2 is highly and even elaborately structured. The many attempts at division into hemistichs and strophes from E. Lohmeyer's to the more recent attempts of M. D. Hooker, J. Murphy-O'Connor and even the 26th edition of the Nestle-Aland *Novum Testamentum Graece* (1979) demonstrate both their persistence and their partial failure, each successive attempt being in its own way a modification and a refutation of the preceding ones. Most recently, however, the attempt to utilize structural criticism in the analysis of the pericope has introduced a new and—I believe in this instance—a valuable methodology into the discussion. The article by A. Spreafico mentioned above subjects Philippians 2:6-11 to such analysis. It does so by first structuring the pericope on the *livello formale* by isolating the subjects of the dominant verbs—the *hos (Christos Iēsous)* of verses 6 to 8 and the *ho theos* of verses 9 to 11—and the principal particles of *ouch, alla,* and *dio* in verses 6, 7, and 9 respectively.[15] As a result of this analysis, the pericope appears made up of two parts: the action of Christ in the first and the action of God in the second, both articulated by the *dio* (therefore) of verse 9.

This structure[16] reveals that the pericope itself is constructed around two fundamental oppositions of the *theos-kyrios (God-Lord) and the doulos-anthrōpos* (slave-man).[17] A semantic analysis of these opposed structures, moreover, discloses two corresponding systems: one spatial (above/below) and the other qualitative (divinity/humanity; power/dependence; and life/mortality).[18] The correspondence between these two opposing spheres is evident: the *theos-kyrios* is the sphere of divinity, of power, and of life above; the *doulos-anthrōpos* is the sphere of humanity, of dependence, and of mortality here below. Thus, the situation of the *doulos* is that of true humanity with all its consequences and specifically with the consequence of obedience to the destiny of all humanity, death.[19] This process toward death, moreover, is a closed one, *mechri* ("unto" of verse 8) indicating the end of a process. This closed process, in turn, is opposed to the process of the *doxa* (glory) which is open and dynamic (*eis*), a consequence of the new condition of the *kyrios*. This is why God is rightly called *patēr* (Father), for it is he who brings the dead to life by conferring the dignity of the *kyrios* on the *doulos-anthrōpos*. Consequently, the whole movement is one that is open toward the new and continuous manifestation of the *doxa* of the Father: "to the glory of God the Father."[20]

This rather lengthy summary of Spreafico's structural analysis is deemed necessary because it shows the hymn to be fundamentally bi-partite and not—as a three-stage Christology interpretation would seem to require—tri-partite. Its dual oppositions derive from its constitutive elements rather than from any preconceived structural binary system, which often seems so arbitrary in the structural analyses of biblical texts. The whole composition of the pericope moves inexorably toward its climax, the *eis doxan theou patros*. If we choose to call it a "hymn" then it is one that hymns the glory of the Father,[21] else its first part (verses 6 to 8) would remain a truncated statement, almost a dangling subordinate clause.

II. The Theological Exegesis

It would be fair to say, I believe, that the primary interest of the hymn and the principal source of most of its exegetical problems have been and continue to be its triple stage Christology: the pre-existent Son, the incarnate Christ, and the exalted Lord. There is no denying the fact that the pericope lends itself quite readily to such a *prima facie* interpretation. The problems that ensue—and they are by no means small or negligible—arise, in large measure, out of this interpretation. Even the various attempts at stichometry are ultimately attributable to this tripartite Christology. This is all too comprehensible for those who read the hymn against the background of their confession that this only Son of the Father, who became man, suffered, was crucified and died for us, and who rose again from the dead, is now seated at the right hand of the Father.

To speak in this context of a three-stage Christology is, if not altogether satisfactory, at least convenient. It keeps in mind that Christ was from all eternity the pre-existent Son of God, who took flesh and came down to earth, suffered and died on the cross, and finally rose again from the dead and ascended to heaven whence he originally came. Much as we are accustomed to this way of thinking, we have to keep in mind that the order of these assertions in their original formulations was quite the reverse from that to which our credal affirmations have accustomed us. It took a good deal of time to reach the "three-stage" formulation. During his own lifetime Jesus was addressed

as "Master" or "Teacher" or "Son of David" or perhaps
even as "King" and "Messiah." It was after his resurrection
that his followers addressed him with the titles of exaltation, such as "Lord" and "Son of God." In this "second
stage" so called it soon became evident that if he is Lord
now he must have been so in his lifetime. The evangelists,
of course, have accustomed us to this retrojection of the
titles of his exaltation into the public ministry of Jesus. It
was later that the consciousness dawned upon the believers that he, who is now Lord and Son of God, who was so in
his lifetime, must have been so from all eternity, that is, he
must have had a pre-existence prior to his coming into the
world. It is arguable, however, whether this "third stage"
of pre-existence is already to be found in our New Testament as, for instance, in the Prologue to John's Gospel. But
it is quite an open question whether such "pre-existence"
could be found anywhere in the genuine Pauline writings.

To take a statement like that in the Philippians hymn
and deal with it as though the pre-existence is to be taken
for granted should give us pause. To assert the hymn in
Philippians 2 to be pre-Pauline, or to claim for it or for its
retroversion into Aramaic a Jewish origin, would require
far more evidence than has hitherto emerged in the ongoing discussion of its pre-Pauline origins. The question,
of course, remains whether Paul speaks of Christ's pre-
existence at all in any of the genuinely Pauline letters. This
is neither to deny Christ's pre-existence nor to belittle
Paul's Christology as, so to speak, a "lower" Christology. It
is simply to take stock of the evidence as it exists and not to
read into it subsequent credal formulations. But, whether
Paul's writings speak of the pre-existence or not, the interpreter's presuppositions would inevitably have far-
reaching consequences for the exegesis of the hymn. This
is ultimately what lies behind the endless debates and
discussions of the *ouch harpagmon* of verse 6, the *res rapta/
rapienda* theories used to explain it,[22] and the meaning of

ekenōsen in verse 7.[23] Of course, such a pre-existence interpretation would always raise the question of what could
possibly be given him who had everything from all eternity. Even the discussion of whether the Old Testament
background of the hymn reflects Isaiah's Suffering Servant or the Book of Wisdom[24] is ultimately reducible to the
question about how the pre-existence itself is to be
understood.

If, however, we take the bipartite structural analysis
of the hymn and regard it as a statement only of Christ's
life here on earth and of his subsequent resurrection-
exaltation, then the discussion of the implications of *hyper-
ypsōsen* (highly exalted) in verse 9, and the debate on
whether and how Paul speaks of Christ's exaltation can
reach a hopeless impasse unless we can resolve definitively
the question of the origin of the hymn. As recently as 1979,
E. Lupieri[25] has argued that the hymn, "its vocabulary,
structure, syntax and content" are Pauline. But, whether it
is original with Paul or whether its origin is Jewish or
Hellenistic-Gnostic or even a "Christian Midrash,"[26] the
fact remains that it is, in its present state, without any of
the proposed conjectural emendations, a part of the letter
to the Philippians. It is by no means loosely added to its
present context but firmly embedded in it.[27] As such, the
hymn can be read and interpreted as we would read and
interpret any part of a Pauline letter. Even if it did have an
independent existence prior to its incorporation into Philippians, its present context and its meaning within the
context have to be respected. Its radication within this
context is far more firmly secured than, say, any of the
hymns that punctuate the Lukan infancy narratives (Lk.
1-2). You cannot very well remove it from its present
context and leave that part of Philippians intelligible as you
could, for instance, remove the Magnificat from Luke 1
and leave the flow of the narrative uninterrupted and
intelligible.[28] Even if—as is quite likely—Philippians is a

composite letter, this pericope belongs firmly to the part where it is found.

This being the case, what does the hymn say in its present context? It is, first of all, part of a typically Pauline *paraklēsis*, a message of consolation and exhortation to love, to communion (*koinōnia*) in the Spirit, to affection and sympathy:

> So if there is any encouragement in Christ, any incentive of love, any participation in the Spirit, any affection and sympathy (Phil. 2:1).

By the very repetition of *phron-* in its various forms and combinations, moreover, the accent of this paraenesis is clearly on being of "one mind" (*to hen phronountes*) (verse 2), on having a "humble mind" (*tapeinophrosynē*) (verse 3), on "having this mind (*phroneite*) among yourselves, which is yours in Christ Jesus" (verse 5). It is an exhortation to a right mental attitude, a Christian outlook and a Christ-like frame of mind that goes counter to the Philippians'—or any reader's—innate "selfishness and conceit" to the extent of regarding others as "better than yourselves" (2:3). This is what makes, not only accord and harmony between Christians possible, but what secures that genuine and unaffected love which looks out "not only to his own interests, but also to the interests of others" (2:4). This is what it means to have that mind which is "yours in Christ Jesus" (2:5).

The words that follow this statement in verse 5 explain the exhortation, else they mean nothing at all in their present context, however sublime and exalted their meaning in a pre-Pauline original might have been. The words that follow *hos* ("who") in verse 6 are explanatory of what this mind "which is yours in Christ Jesus" means. They are not an invitation to "imitate" him, nor are they the elaboration of an "ethic," but the exposition of an attitude which is characteristically Christ's and which ought to mark the

Christian life as specifically Christian, i.e., the Christian life as made possible by the life, death *and* resurrection of Christ Jesus. As can be seen from such passages as Romans 14:5-9; 2 Corinthians 8:9, 5:21; or Galatians 4:4-5, such a mode of exhortation is typically Pauline.

What then does the hymn say about this "mind" which ought to be the Philippians' "in Christ Jesus"? In its first part (verses 6 to 8), its description of the condition of the *doulos-anthrōpos* here below, it makes two parallel statements: the first,

> though he was in the form of God, did not count equality with God a thing to be grasped, but emptied himself, taking the form of a slave (*morphēn doulou*);

and the second

> being born in the likeness of men (*en homoiōmati anthrōpōn*) and being found in human form (*hōs anthrōpos*) he humbled himself and became obedient unto death, even death on a cross.

Thus, one can argue that, like the "first Adam" (1 Cor. 15:22, 45; and see 15:47-49, 15:22; and Rom. 5:14, 12, 17), this man was "in the form of God," in God's image and likeness (Gn. 1:26, cf. 3:22); but that, unlike the first Adam, the man Jesus, rather than grasp for equality with God ("You will be like God" in Gn. 3:5), "emptied himself," assuming the lowest station among men, that of a condemned and crucified slave.

The contrast is not merely between Adam's pride and Christ's humility, but between the rebellious disobedience of the former and the self-sacrificing obedience to God of the latter. This is the contrast that is heightened by the parallel statements of his "being born in the likeness of men...being found in human form" and the "humbled himself and became obedient unto death," not to any ordinary death, but to a death reserved for the lowest of humanity's low, a death on the cross. This humility, obe-

dience and death on the cross explain the extent of the
kenosis, the "emptying out" of himself. He freely and willingly, in other words, embraced the lowest and most despised position among men: not just a slave, but a condemned slave, not a mere condemnation to an ordinary
death, but a condemnation to that execrable death on a
criminal's cross.

This is what gives the *dio* (therefore) of verse 9 its force.
The totality of this humility, of this complete obedience, of
this basest of deaths is what leads up to the *dio*. This
"therefore God has highly exalted him" (2:9) is what provides the clue of intelligibility to the whole series of events.
To this extent, E. Käsemann is right to regard the hymn as
a series of events of salvation.[29] The bestowal upon Christ
Jesus of "the name which is above every name" (verse 9)
and the consequent confession of his Lordship (verse 11)
are what make not only Christian worship[30] "reasonable"
(Rm. 12:1) but the call to Christian life both intelligible and
possible. The Lordship of Christ, his universal dominion
(verse 10) and the bestowal upon him of "the name which
is above every name" have but one sole and unique aim:
"the glory of God the Father." The *kenosis*-humility-
obedience and the exaltation-lordship-dominion are to
that one sole end, "the glory of God the Father," who gave
true life to him who died ignominiously on the cross.

III. The Paraenesis

The consequence of this train of events, the "Therefore,
my beloved..." in verse 13, is a corresponding Christian
obedience that is aware of the constant and almost insur-
mountable temptation to reiterate the gesture of the first
Adam. The "fear and trembling" (verse 12) with which the
faithful are exhorted to work out their salvation is not so
much that of the severity of the just Judge as that of the
self-knowledge of the Christian. It is the lucidity of self-
knowlege that causes the "fear and trembling," not the

awesome expectation of a judgment pronounced by an austere and stern Judge. The true Christian knows from experience that the temptation to "be like God" is constantly there, often under the holiest of guises. But, Paul hastens to add, "God is at work in you, both to will and to work for his good pleasure" (2:13). Thus, the "to the glory (*doxa*) of God the Father" in verse 11 and his "good pleasure (*eudokia*)" in verse 13 bind the paraenesis intimately to the hymn. What Christ did in obedience to God was for the glory of the Father; what the Christian does in having the "mind" which is his in Christ Jesus is to the very same end: the good pleasure of God. Consequently, what Philippians 2:6-11 states is both the foundation and the principle of Christian life in Christ.

It was said above that this paraenesis is an exhortation to an attitude, to a frame of mind. This is not what is generally understood by an "ethic," though such an interpretation tends to be classified as "ethical." The paraenesis, moreover, is not an invitation to "imitate" Christ, either in his obedience to the Father, which is unique, or in his way of dying, which is rare. It is rather an exhortation, a *paraklēsis*, to set no store by that all too human striving to be "like God," but to take exactly the opposite attitude, seeking not one's fulfillment but rather emptying oneself out, striving not for one's own exaltation but embracing the lowliness of a slave, working not to gain one's life but to lose it in loving service of others.[31] It is, therefore, an invitation to live by a standard and according to a norm that is Christ's, not Adam's, one that is diametrically opposed to the self-centered aspirations of this world's "folly" (1 Cor. 1:23-25).

The various attempts at interpreting the Philippians hymn have always found—and quite rightly—a triple-stage Christological reading extremely problematic in its application to the life of the Christian. Such an application would, of course, be necessitated by the context of the hymn, by the verses that immediately precede and follow it in Philippians 2, and especially by the more immediate imperative of Philippians 2:5, "Have this mind among you...." If in the triple scheme the pre-existence could serve to heighten the humility and the abasement of the second stage, and could thus be regarded as a call to Christian humility—along lines similar to St. Augustine's "God has so humbled himself, and yet man is so proud," the exaltation itself would remain, and continue to remain, quite refractory to the paraenetic exhortation. The Christian is not, and could not be, called upon to "follow" or to "imitate" this particular stage.

The paraenesis of Philippians 2 is not unique in the writings of St. Paul, nor is its pattern rare. In addition to the paraenesis in Romans 12, one might consider those in Second Corinthians:

> For you know the grace of our Lord Jesus Christ, that though he was rich, yet for your sake he became poor, so that by his poverty you might become rich (8:9);

and

> For our sake he made him to be sin who knew no sin, so that in him we might become the righteousness of God (5:21);

or that in Galatians:

> But when the time had fully come, God sent his Son, born of woman, born under the law, to redeem those who were under the law, so that we might receive adoption as sons (4:4-5).[32]

This "becoming rich" far beyond the dreams of our innate avarice, this God-conferred "righteousness" far more genuine than all the strivings after holiness and perfection, and this "adoption as sons," a far truer title to divinity than all our efforts to be "like unto God"—these are the true and abiding gifts of the redemption we have in Christ Jesus.

If the Philippians hymn calls upon Christians to let go

the deceptive security of self-fulfillment, self-realization, self-assertiveness, such a call is not an end in itself. It is but the way—the only unfailingly Christian and Christ-like way—to enter into our true glory, to be what we were made to be, through Christ, to the glory of God the Father.

NOTES

[1]R. P. Martin, *Carmen Christi. Philippians 2:5-11 in Recent Interpretation and in the Setting of Early Christian Worship*, Society of New Testament Studies Monograph Series 4 (Cambridge University Press, 1967), p. 24.

[2]Ambrogio Spreafico, "*Theos/anthrōpos*: Filippesi 2, 6-11," *Rivista Biblica* 28 (1980) 407-415.

[3]See above note 1.

[4]Jean Carmignac, "L'Importance de la place d'une négation: *ouch harpagmon hēgēsato* (Philippiens II. 6)," *New Testament Studies* 18 (1971-72) 131-166.

[5]Pierre Grelot, "Deux notes critiques sur Philippiens 2, 6-11," *Biblica* 54 (1973) 169-186; and see his previous two articles: "Deux expressions difficiles de Philippiens 2, 6-7," *Biblica* 53 (1972) 495-507; and "La valeur de *ouk...alla...*dans Philippiens 2, 6-7," *Biblica* 54 (1973) 25-42.

[6]Morna D. Hooker, "Philippians 2:6-11," in *Jesus und Paulus*. Festschrift für Werner Georg Kümmel zum 70. Geburtstag, edited by E. Earl Ellis and Erich Grässer (Göttingen: Vandenhoeck & Ruprecht, 1975), pp. 151-164.

[7]Jerome Murphy-O'Connor, "Christological Anthropology in Phil. II, 6-11," *Revue Biblique* 83 (1976) 25-50.

[8]See above note 2.

[9]R. P. Martin, *Carmen Christi*, p. 24.

[10]L. Cerfaux, *Le Christ dans la théologie de saint Paul*, 2nd ed. rev., Lectio Divina 6 (Paris: Cerf, 1951), p. 284; see also R. P. Martin, *Carmen Christi*, p. 56.

[11]L. Cerfaux, *Le Christ*, p. 284.

[12]See R. P. Martin, *Carmen Christi*, chapter 3, pp. 42-62.

[13]Ernst Lohmeyer, *Kyrios Jesus. Eine Untersuchung zu Phil. 2, 5-11*, 2nd ed. (Heidelberg: Carl Winter, 1961 reprint of the edition of 1928), pp. 5-6.

[14]M. D. Hooker, p. 158.

[15]A. Spreafico, p. 408.

[16]*Ibid.*, p. 411.

[17]*Ibid.*

[18]*Ibid.*, p. 412.

[19]*Ibid.*, p. 413.

[20]*Ibid.*, p. 413f.

[21]See recent views on the recurrence of an antiphonal response which, psalm-like, punctuates the whole hymn. See George Howard, "Phil. 2:6-11 and the Human Christ," *Catholic Biblical Quarterly* 40 (1978) 368-387, especially p. 378 and footnote 30 with its reference to K. Gamber, "Der Christus-Hymnus im Philipperbrief in liturgiege-schichtlicher Sicht," *Biblica* 51 (1970) 369-376.

[22]See the articles of J. Carmignac and M. D. Hooker cited above.

[23]P. Henry, "Kénose," *Dictionnaire de la Bible.* Supplément, volume V (Paris: Letouzey et Ané, 1957), columns 7-161, especially columns 12-14 and 28-29.

[24]See J. Murphy-O'Connor's article cited above and Dieter Georgi, "Der vorpaulinische Hymnus Phil 2, 6-11," in *Zeit und Geschichte.* Dankes-gabe an Rudolf Bultmann zum 80. Geburtstag, edited by Erich Dinkler (Tübingen: J. C. B. Mohr, 1964), pp. 263-293.

[25]Edmondo Lupieri, "La morte di Croce. Contributi per un'analisi di *Fil.* 2, 6-11," *Rivista Biblica* 27 (1979) 271-311.

[26]Frédéric Manns, "Un hymne judéo-chrétien: Philippiens 2, 6-11," *Euntes Docete* 29 (1976) 259-290.

[27]See M. D. Hooker's article cited above on the connections with what precedes and with what follows the pericope, pp. 152-153.

[28]See, for example, Raymond E. Brown, *The Birth of the Messiah* (Garden City, NY: Doubleday, 1977), pp. 339-365. "[The canticles in Luke 2] seem to be appendages and can be easily excised so that the reader would never miss them" (p. 244).

[29]Ernst Käsemann, "A Critical Analysis of Philippians 2:5-11," *Journal for Theology and the Church* 5 (1968) 45-88. "In the plethora of expressions God's act of salvation is celebrated. And the salvation-event is shown here in its characteristic aspect" (p. 65).

[30]See note 21 above.

[31]Compare the Synoptic theme of "whoever would save his life will lose it..." in Mark 8:35 and par.; Matthew 10:39; and Luke 17:33.

[32]M. D. Hooker has called this pattern a pattern of "interchange." See her "Interchange in Christ," *Journal of Theological Studies,* New Series 22 (1971) 349-361.

CHRIST AND THE
CONTEMPLATIVE EXPERIENCE

Jean Leclercq, OSB
*(Monk of the Abbey of St.-Maurice,
Clervaux, Luxembourg)*

I: Growth, Purification, and Liberation

Contemplation comes from a Greek word meaning *to see.*
But we do *not* see, so what is meant by this word? There is a
Christian reality that has its source in the New Testament:
"Jesus contemplating on the mountain" as we read in the
documents of Vatican II. We have to consider what is
special compared to other forms of the search for a God, an
Absolute, a Supreme Being. Now, *what is special or specific is
precisely the Christian experience, the experience of Jesus Christ.*

Jesus is the contemplator of the Father in the Spirit for
the Church, and when we participate in his contemplation,
we participate in his mission of salvation for the Church.
This experience supposes a detachment, a separation
freely made, and consequently an act of liberation for
ourselves and for the entire world. I will try to make this
more clear by going into greater detail.

First, what do we know of the contemplative experience
of Jesus? Christology of the past and the present helps us
to get some idea of it.

The experience of Jesus' contemplation of God is the
Christian experience par excellence. Jesus did not speak of
God like someone reciting a theory learned beforehand.
The moment he became man, one of us, Jesus who pre-
existed in God's plan, began a human experience, discover-
ing what it is to be united with God, to be Son of God as he
is. He did not teach ideas but he explained an experience he
lived which was essentially living God like his father,

"Abba, Father," and all he can do subsequently is to give us
the interpretation of this experience. "No one has ever
seen God; it is only the Son who is nearest to the Father's
heart who has made him known." Jesus saw God as his
Father and explained him to us word for word. This is his
Gospel, his message, as expressed in the different texts
that have come down to us and are interpretations that
could not have been written if Jesus had not often spoken
of God as his Father. This is all John's Gospel but we find it
also in Luke (10:21-22) a passage that is so much like John
that some say it is a stray text of his. There and elsewhere,
Jesus testifies that he sees God as his Father. He speaks of
experience not merely of a beautiful theory. He was living
with God whom he calls Abba, "papa" with all that this
connotes of union, intimacy, dependence, acceptation, love
and the security of knowing that he is equally accepted and
loved by his Father.

Because Jesus was the contemplator par excellence, all
experience of prayer and of contemplation is a participation in the experience of Jesus, a continuation of it. It
makes present in us, and presents to the world through us,
the experience of Jesus, which was a certain transparence
or "shining through" of the presence of the Father.

Now we are talking about a *human* experience. Jesus
becomes man, foetus, baby, child, adult; he grows. Like
every other human experience, that of Jesus developed as
time went on. He "became" man. But he was likewise Jesus
of Nazareth, situated in space and in time, the son of Mary
and Joseph. His development was gradual, painful and
normal. He experienced progressively, but in a privileged
manner unique in the world, what it is to be united to *his*
Father; a supreme light, absolute and transparent, gave
him the total certitude of his union with the Father and his
mission among men.

But the knowledge he had of himself and his resolve to
accomplish his mission remained subject to the laws of

human development. The fact that his understanding of himself was progressive explains the terms he uses in speaking of himself. One of the benefits of contemporary Christology is the light it throws on the human aspect of Christ's development. The problem today is to reconcile this more intense revelation of the humanity of Jesus with his divinity, to understand that there is no contradiction between the two.

This mystery of his growth has several consequences. Jesus had not only the knowledge or revelation of his Father, but also the experience of the limitations of his knowledge and of the transparence of God in him. And this implied on his part an acceptation of these limitations and a purification, a renunciation of his own human expectations. His own future remained, to a certain degree, obscure, and he had to accept this. His understanding of the Kingdom was, for some length of time, mixed with images that only gradually faded away in the light of events in which the Spirit led him to discern signs of God.

Jesus awaited the Kingdom of God with absolute confidence. Open to the will of his Father, he continually sought to know what it was. Within his total trust and experience there was room for a certain growth, hence a certain renouncement. Some texts lead us to think that he also expected an immediate Kingdom during his own lifetime. He expected his Father to get him out of difficulty should need arise. But events were to prove that his Father was not to intervene thus. Jesus was rejected and condemned because the Kingdom did not come as expected by those around him. Jesus had to accept the fact that God was not going to defend him against his enemies at the last moment. On the contrary, his Father abandoned him. He was betrayed and delivered into the hands of his enemies. He had to renounce all effectiveness. Current Christology insists on the feeling Jesus had that he had failed. Yet this did not diminish his trust in his Father, his obedience and his interior certitude that his Father loved him. All this he learned through suffering by way of obedience.

His life and even his death appeared to be useless. No visible good resulted from his death. Suffering from being abandoned by his Father, he dies with a prayer commending his soul to Him. His gift is the free gift of himself, the abandoning of himself to the Father for all men. His death is not for the success of some cause but "for God." And as I see it, this is what takes place in the life of a contemplative. Such a life is a constant seeking for God with no other effectiveness than that of prayer. Its real beginning, its source is the contemplative experience of Jesus. Now Jesus had prepared for his ultimate renouncement of all human expectations and normal hopes by a life of persecution willingly accepted. His renunciation was a free act, a liberation from his own projects and expectations, from those of others and also from their pressures. Whence the importance, in the Gospel, of temptations coming from the devil, from the priests, from his family, his disciples, even Peter; temptations resulting from the human representations of the Kingdom that had been announced. All these temptations aimed at restricting his message and his mission, reducing them to merely human hopes.

Jesus really had to suffer temptation, tension between different possibilities. These temptations, these tensions, these hesitations were so many occasions for him to give renewed consent to the Father's will as it became known to him. Jesus clearly stated his absolute autonomy whenever he was tempted, e.g., on the mountain.

This example of liberation from those around him as well as from self, were, like everything else that happened to him, an experience for Jesus, an experience in the Spirit who was always at work in Jesus until the moment he died on the cross.

The assertion of this liberty that enabled him to overcome temptation was not a passing thing. Jesus was always free, but his freedom knew moments of greater intensity and the greatest was the moment of his death. Death is the most terrible thing that happens to a human person but Jesus accepted his, albeit with tears, even tears of blood. It was a freely won victory over temptation. But it was not automatic. Jesus had to keep on repeating his acceptation: "Yes, Father." Jesus prayed to be spared: "Father, if it is possible," but also "not my will, but thine." His own human nature would naturally have desired another solution, but the Spirit gave him the strength to accept God's will, transforming his death into a freely made offering of himself.

And does this not apply to contemplative life with its moments of greater difficulty that vary with each person? In moments of ineffectiveness, one is tempted to seek effectiveness elsewhere than in total abandonment to God. It is the Holy Spirit who makes it possible for us to participate by faith in the experience of Jesus. For Jesus, the experience consisted in knowing that he was with the Father, in remaining faithful to him and to his own mission, despite the fact that he could not satisfy the human expectations of those around him. He accepted the apparently total failure of his mission in order to pay the price of man's salvation. The Holy Spirit alone could make this possible in Jesus just as he alone can make it possible in us in faith, hope, and charity. It is this gift of the Spirit that enables us to enter into the most intimate attitudes of Jesus. We do not have to imitate his culture, but we must reproduce his great fidelity to his Father.

All this supposes that it is possible for millions of people to relive personally the experience of Jesus. Jesus glorified, freed from death, from the limitations of time and space can re-live in each one of us the unlimited life of God, by the power of his Spirit whom he sends continually to his Church and to each one of us. This is the paschal experience his disciples had. Not the experience of some knowledge or reflection such as they had had previously, but a new knowledge given by the Spirit of the Resurrection who now gives it to us. We participate in their experience because they participated in that of Christ. We share his ability to overcome difficulties and doubts and to give our life to God.

The Holy Spirit makes us capable of following the examples of Jesus, not only interiorly and psychologically, but by all our life. We not only contemplate Jesus, we behave like him. His profound experience consists in renouncing the effectiveness of his life and death and this aspect of the life of Christ lies at the heart of contemplative life.

Renouncing all that is not part of God's plan for us! Is this not the meaning of the trials, the purifications, the darkness the spiritual masters have told us about? They all come back to the one thing—the gift, the total abandonment of self to God.

This experience of contemplative life supposes in us, as in Jesus, a continual purification; it is Jesus in us who continues his purification. We have to re-live this experience of Jesus, not as something static, given once and for all, but as a continuing, dynamic experience that develops day by day. It was realized once and for all in Christ, but is given to us initially at our baptism, and again when we are called to religious life, but we have to cultivate and deepen it. Contemplative life favors this experience. Other forms of Christian life may distract one from it but contemplative life continually draws us back to this experience and this is our responsibility as contemplatives. We must take advantage of the way of life the Church prescribes for us in order to live this experience profoundly and not let ourselves become absorbed by disturbing factors or by compensations of any kind. We have to center our minds and hearts only on Jesus and his mysteries, for without this great love, this passion, a cloistered life is a failure, a loss for the individual and for the Church—a truly unhappy life.

A certain obscurity was inherent to the experience of Jesus as it is for the Christian also, and the contemplative experience is nothing other than the Christian experience but more regular, more intense, because more exclusive and favored by certain living conditions. Suffering was a purification necessary for Christ and it remains the very same for Christians, especially for some of them. The contemplative experience is one of freedom; it is an act of freedom that we must make and renew constantly: an act of liberation. All theology of liberation should include these two great realities: martyrdom and the importance of prayer. Jesus freed us all, especially when he gave his life to fulfill God's plan and to show his love for humanity. When, during his Passion, Jesus offered his life at the Last Supper, he freed the world spiritually from all the oppressions resulting from sin. He gave the example of a form of liberation with which we are particularly associated in contemplative life.

II: The Transparency of Christ

How can we participate in the experience of Christ? We must first consider what is meant by having a personal relationship with Christ. How can an historical individual like Jesus have a universal value? Despite the historic distance in time, the centuries that separate us from the period when he lived on earth, how can he have a spiritual presence, and by means of what mediations and intermediaries? Is it possible that the very person of Jesus, his reality and all that he did, can remain present over the years? For being Christian means having a personal relationship with God. How can this be? It also means a personal, spiritual relationship with him not only through the transmission of Scripture which would be of a cultural nature, but a real person-to-person relationship. Nor is it a mere awareness, a psychological phenomenon; it is an interpersonal reality existing between him and each one of us. (All these ideas have been developed by Johannes Heinricks in *Personnliche Beziehung zu Jesus Christus, Skizze zu eines handlangs theoretis hen Christologie in Theologie und Philosophie*, 54 [1979], pp. 65-80.)

Such an interpersonal relationship cannot be of an intellectual order only, an affair of knowledge and reason. It has to be a relation of *love* and *faith* which calls for an acceptation, a *commitment,* a reciprocal "belonging" and fidelity. All that we perceive of ideal human love must be applicable to this relationship, whence the importance of the nuptial metaphor in the tradition of all the great mystical authors such as St. Bernard and St. John of the Cross. It is of this more-than-intellectual relationship that we read in both St. John and St. Paul. The person of Jesus and relations with him must become a transforming reality in the person of the Christian. Jesus who exists, who is real in himself, becomes real and existent in us. Here then, we are dealing with a relational Christology, the real relation there is between Christ and us, between us and Christ as that which saves us. From this comes the relation we find in today's Christology as treated by theologians and by the constant teaching of John Paul II, the relation between anthropology, a just idea of the nature of man, and the meaning, the reality expressed by a relatively new term *pro-existence,* which means—in Christ and in the Christian— the fact of *existing for.* Furthermore, this pro-existence supposes in Christ a *pre-existence.* It is a question of a relation not only to the historic Christ who came, but to the Christ who exists beyond history, forever, and in his eschatological existence.

And this relation can exist only in a free, loving participation in the individuality and universality of Christ. While respecting his individuality, we must assume its meaning, value and efficacy. Jesus is the mediator who, in his person, makes it possible for all mankind to participate in God. The Church really consists of these interpersonal relations with Christ; she is not primarily an institution. The institution results from the reality of these relations. The Church is the unity of life resulting from the relation of all Christians to the one and same personality of Christ. There is reconciliation in Christ in each and all of us, between what is most personal yet common to all.

The Church is the sum total of these personal relations with the One "who enlightens all men coming into this world" as St. John says. And the contemplatives serve the Church only if they favor this personal relationship. She is not there to make an institution function effectively, but to make very real an encounter with God in Three Persons, through Jesus Christ by the Spirit of the Son and the Father. This means participating in the contemplation of God by participating in contemplation of Jesus.

To treat this subject of the contemplative experience of Jesus, we can take as our starting point the key text of St. John 1:9, in the Prologue: "The Word was the true light that enlightens all men, and he was coming into the world," or according to another translation, "Coming into this world, he enlightens all men." Coming into this world, that is, becoming man in Jesus Christ who can say, "I am the way, the truth and the life"; in other words, the sign, the means of manifesting—of revealing God and making him known. Traditional piety has often concentrated on the personal character of the contemplative experience of Jesus, especially of each one of us, and we must respect this but join this personal consideration with reflection on the objectivity of universal salvation for all men coming into the world.

For many years we were more familiar with what were known as "Christologies from above" that showed Jesus in the light of what we know of the Word through St. John in his Prologue, and through ancient tradition which insists a great deal on the Divinity of Jesus. But in the last fifteen years or so, we have come to put more emphasis on a "Christology from below" based on more specific consideration of the human life of Jesus. And just as there used to be a tendency to over-emphasize the aspect "from above," there is now a tendency to exaggerate the aspect "from below." Fortunately, in more recent years, we have recaptured a better balance in Christology that reconciles all the acquired knowledge of Tradition insisting on the divinity of Jesus, with all the acquisitions of recent biblical sciences insisting on his humanity, his life here below. This is done especially in what is termed a "Christology of or *in* the Spirit," which shows the important part played by the Spirit of God, present and active in the man Jesus. God made man in Jesus Christ reveals and manifests himself in and through a humanity that he respects but also elevates. God manifested himself in the experience of Jesus. Jesus' experience is essentially the experience of being with the Father, of receiving everything from the Father in the Spirit, of giving everything to the Father through the Spirit, and of receiving everything from the Father in order to give everything, all that he is, to us.

Now it seems to me that the best way to express the reality of the experience of Jesus in himself and in his members is by evoking the idea of transparency. In and through Jesus, men could sense God. God could be seen in and through Jesus and we see this in the Gospel, especially in John's where we are given the dialogue between Jesus and his Father in the Spirit. But this is likewise apparent in many of the texts of the Synoptics where we really assist at the prayer of Jesus; prayer that is the expression of his experience, his enthusiasm, his love, his acceptation and his suffering. These prayers, reflecting the experience of Jesus, respect both his humanity with its limitations and his union with the Word—the Incarnate Word, one with the Father in the Spirit. It is very difficult to speak of the experience of Jesus. In one of his later books, *Of Grace and of the Humanity of Jesus Christ,* Maritain advances an interesting idea. He reminds us that modern psychology consists in bringing out notions of the conscious and the subconscious levels. The latter includes the unconscious, the subconscious and the pre-conscious, and finally the conscious. Psychology insists particularly on all this infra-conscious.

But there is also a *supra-conscious* manifested in certain spiritual experiences such as those of love, of art; also in the experience of prayer reaching a maximum in the experience of Christ. Jesus Christ is man, with the limitations of humanity, particularly a certain ignorance. But at the same time, he is personally united with God and constantly penetrated by the Spirit from whom he receives profound charisms. At the very beginning of his career, and even of his conscious existence, these charisms give him a knowledge— at least general—of his mission as well as a certitude of his privileged union with the Father. Maritain compares the humanity of Jesus to a sort of transparent, translucent screen, a sort of frosted glass. Through an unpolished glass we cannot see the sun but we receive some of its light and heat. Something similar took place in Jesus. His humanity received a real but limited knowledge of his union with the Father and consequently, of his mission. There was then, transparency; a transparency that increased, manifesting itself at certain moments, by his mission itself, then on the cross, and to the higher degree at the instant of the resurrection.

This is but a rapid perception of the experience of Jesus. It is important because it determines the traits of our contemplative experience, its certitude and its share of obscurity. Let us now consider the transparence of God and of Jesus among men.

God made himself transparent, that is, "seeable through"; he let himself be seen through Jesus. Jesus let us see God in him. What do we mean by participating in the prayer of

Christ, in his life, in his person, his activities, his offering of himself to his Father? How can we have a personal relationship with Christ? This is a delicate anthropological problem. What are the ingredients, the factors, the elements of this personal relationship? We can restrict them to three:

1. First there must be *an historic and objective relationship* with him, founded on the facts, the actual happenings, the words that have come down to us through the exegesis of texts that speak of him, chiefly through Scripture. These are precise facts of the past, things we *know*, that can be the basis of a relationship of knowledge and remembrance but not of faith and love in a sharing of life with him. However, this relationship of knowledge is indispensable, and it justifies all that is of the order of *lectio*, of contemplative study by which we apply ourselves to learning all that we possibly can of what Jesus really was. This knowledge, necessary as it is, is nevertheless insufficient. We must go further and deeper until knowledge opens the door to the *experience* of Jesus which is possible only if we *believe* in the doctrine of the Word incarnate in him. St. John bases all his Gospel on the person of the Word in Jesus.

2. Secondly, there must be *a participation by faith and love* which alone permits a subjective, existential relation with Jesus, completing the participation and relationship of knowledge. This relationship of love is one of commitment, generosity and fervor; in a word, of *faith*. By faith, every human person can enter into real union with Christ and with all human persons by participating in him who is "the true Light that enlightens all men." And if every man can have this participation, even before the Incarnation, it must be because the Word existed, pre-existed the individual, Jesus of Nazareth. This implies two things:

a) the identity of the Word and of Jesus. Jesus and the Word are united; they are one. He is the Incarnate Word.

b) through Jesus, all can participate in the Word. There must be at one and the same time, communication of the Word in Christ, of Christ in all men, and of all men among themselves and with him. Jesus is the significant means of communicating God to man. He is the mediator. Hence, the need of an exact knowledge of the pre-existence of Jesus, in the sense that the divine Word, the personal Word existed in God before all creation and in view of creation and of the history of salvation. This is in accord with the oldest Christology. From all eternity, the Word is orientated to his union with humanity, to his Incarnation. Therefore pre-existence does not mean only that the Divinity of the Word existed before the Incarnation, in which case there would be no need to speak of pre-existence since we know the Divinity is eternal. Nor does it imply that Jesus, man, would have had a previous existence as God-man. No, the only Son, pre-existing in God, began and stopped existing in time. But a God-Man unity between God and man existed before the appearing of the historic individuality of Jesus.

Now this real, total relation to God and to all creation in the Word can be deduced only from the individual Jesus who revealed it. From all eternity, there existed in God a real image of the mystery, a pre-formation of the mystery of the personality of Jesus revealed retrospectively by Jesus. Creation finds its own unity, not in itself, but in a divine and personal principle—divine because personal—which makes it a sign of the unity of the cosmos. According to St. John, he who is the Absolute, lets himself be found in the relative, the temporal, the non-absolute: "Something which has existed since the beginning, that we have heard, and we have seen with our own eyes; that we have watched and touched with our hands: the Word who is life" (1 Jn. 1). This is the mystery of the Incarnation. This Word of Life had already, from all eternity, a relation with all men. It inclined all men to Jesus Christ. Thus, every human

being received from Jesus his understanding of the Incarnate Word; his understanding, that is, the meaning it had
for him, the answer to the fundamental question, "Who
am I as a human person?" What can I know about myself?
For what can I hope? Here we perceive that this *pre-existence*
of the Incarnate Word in Jesus Christ is at the root of
the universal *pro-existence* of Jesus Christ manifesting the
condescendence of God, and even what some call God's
"humility." This pro-existence means that God in Jesus
exists *for*. He takes on the form of slave for mankind: he
became incarnate, dying for us. He gave his life for us,
rising from the dead for our justification, and the Epistle
to the Hebrews shows us that even now he intercedes for
us praying eternally for us. Jesus has an existence for us
that shows us the meaning of our own existence which is
to live for others. Accepting this pro-existence, this overcoming of ourselves for others, participating in Jesus' pro-
existence, supposes a total conversion on our part, a
renouncing of the limitations of our selfishness, a liberation that extends our capacity for loving to the whole
world that Jesus saves.

It is this pre-existence that was manifested in the experience that Jesus had: He acknowleged that he existed by
the Father, for the Father and for us; and those who have
experienced God are aware of this. They have had the
experience of what I call (for want of a better word) the
transparence of God in Jesus. In this context, this word means
"to show oneself through," so we have God showing himself in and through Jesus.

3. This brings us to the third point, the interpersonal,
real, objective, experimental *relation*, the total and definitive *meeting* of God with men in Jesus Christ: a revealing
transparence made possible by the presence of the Word in
Jesus and by the action of the Spirit given by God. Here we
must first consider what was the personal meeting of Jesus
with his contemporaries, and then what it is for us since

that time. In the first case, we have to deal with the time before his Resurrection and then the period that has followed it.

Before the Resurrection, there was in Jesus a certain shining through or transparence of God whom he called his Father. His own experience of the presence of God within himself was carried over into transparence for others. The Gospels abound in signs and proofs of this transparence perceived not only by the disciples but also by the generality of Christ's contemporaries. These have been interpreted by tradition. In the Breviary there used to be a lesson by St. Ambrose in which he said that in Jesus there was a sort of attracting force like a magnet. He sent out beams of light, and anyone who reads the Gospel in sincerity of heart cannot help feeling that it contains a beautiful transparence of God. This transparence grew, developed and became evidence for those who accepted it with faith and love that finally evolved into absolute faith after purification by Christ's apparent failure, hence, after his Resurrection. This same transparence was rejected and hated by some. The very fact of accepting or refusing Jesus as both God and man—man whom one could see, and God of whom one could catch a glimpse through him—hinged on this transparence. Some accepted, some rejected, but all perceived. It is the transparence itself that they recognized which caused rejection by some because it was not the brilliantly striking "shining through" they had expected. They would not give up their own personal expectations in order to accept the transparence of God offered to them in Jesus. Therefore, even before the Resurrection, there was a transparence of God in Jesus which explains the attachment and even the faith of the apostles and the disciples, both men and women. But this transparence had to be accepted just as it was, at the cost of a purification of motives and expectations, and a detachment from personal hopes. This perfectible transparence attained its perfection in the experience of the Resurrection, principle and model of all experience of Christian faith.

What was this experience of the Resurrection? The failure of Jesus, his crucifixion, his death, his catastrophic departure caused those who believed in him to reflect on this Jesus whom they had known as man and as a transparent sign of God. This reflection made possible by the Spirit, was in the nature of an event, a new spiritual experience of the permanent presence of Jesus. They understood that Jesus had been and still was a transparent sign of God, but in an absolute, clear and definitive manner, *glorious* in a word. He was raised up and glorified. At what precise moment, where and how did this paschal event take place for each one of them? This has not been made clear to us. The texts of the New Testament give us to understand that the experience differed according to the witnesses: Peter, James, John, Thomas, the disciples of Emmaus. . . . Paul gives a different historical-psychological description, but everyone had the experience one way or another. This young Rabbi who for three years had charmed, surprised, shocked, and scandalized them, arousing their wonder and love, was still there. After his failure he was alive. They had lost faith and hope as we see by the words of the disciples on their way to Emmaus: "We had hoped. . .and now three days have passed and nothing has happened. . . ." They had lost faith and hope but not love, and it is love that opens the eyes of faith and hope. They recognized him. The experience of the Resurrection consists in recognizing the risen Jesus. They knew him once more. He was the same Jesus but they knew him in a new way, rediscovering him more profoundly. The story of this man they had known, their awareness of his mission, of the doctrine he had taught, all this they now experienced as belonging to divine eternity. Jesus had pre-existed and now was to exist forever, after his paschal rehabilitation.

Such is faith in the Resurrection, this acknowledging of

Jesus. Over and above the first transparence of God in his humanity, there was now a new knowledge, still "shining through" and yet not a revelation of all his glory: a recognition of his divinity and of his paschal victory. Now, Christian faith consists in sharing this experience, in preserving and developing it, also in reflecting on it. The experience of faith is the continuation in us, by the action of the same Spirit, of that experience lived by the witnesses of the Resurrection. It is always a matter of recognizing and acknowledging Jesus living eternally through and beyond the transparence of God in the man Jesus. This direct and visible manifestation to the witnesses of his pre-paschal existence, then to the witnesses of his post-paschal existence, comes to us by what they said of it, by what the Church has handed down to us and still continues to teach. We have to acknowledge, admit and accept the fact that there is more in this than meets the eye. We must accept and love this living man Jesus, living still as he lived before and living now in glory and power in the *doxa*. His glory is now total and his power is present in the Eucharist which contains an anticipation of his eschatological presence. Already in these transformed sacred elements, the transformation of the world to come is anticipated. This man Jesus, now living in glory, this son of God united to his Father, gives us the Spirit of the Father and the Son. The first power he received at the very instant of his Resurrection, from the moment he took his place at the right hand of the Father, was to send forth the Spirit as he did during his first apparition on Easter Sunday. And his Spirit makes it possible for us to recognize him.

Our act of faith is thus a continuation of the paschal experience, and the activity of prayer is the first expression of it. Praying is accepting the transparence of God in Jesus as we now know it in Scripture; consenting, adoring, giving thanks and placing all our trust in him. Hope, abandonment, obedience, offering, supplication are all phases of the same paschal experience lived by the first witnesses and continuing in us. And contemplative life is a life organized so that this experience may be as uninterrupted as possible. But this act of faith, this life of prayer requires endeavor, detachment, constant acceptance of a certain obscurity in the transparence. This is the essential asceticism of contemplative life that has no other purpose but the practice of union with the risen Jesus and with the Spirit who unites us to the Father. In a special and permanent way, contemplatives witness to these mysteries. They are Christians who accept this transparence with the obscurity that is part of it. In us, as in Jesus, as in Mary and as in all his witnesses, the experience of his Resurrection includes an experience of death to self, the renunciation of all human expectations, all hope other than that which comes from God, all selfishness, all attachment to self. And this twofold aspect of this resurrection experience—renouncement to self and recognition of the transparence of Jesus—is not only and primarily of the order of recognition or knowledge; it is of the nature of things which have to be lived through—actually, a death; the death that Jesus accepted for himself, death that he requires of us, death to self that must be part of our life. We have to live the death of Christ, and all that makes us live death to self makes us resurrect in a very concrete manner. Everything that in our personal life, our common life, makes us die—the daily mortifications, often small but continual, which are very real—are occasions to make us live anew, and in this way all the difficulties of contemplative life take on a lofty meaning. Why so many little, apparently insignificant things? Because without them there would be no experience of resurrection. It is by all these little mortifications that day by day, as St. Paul says, I die to self, I rise again and make mine the Resurrection of Christ.

This interpersonal meeting or relationship with Jesus is an interpersonal experience *in the Church*, not only of me with him but of all of us with him, of all the Church and in particular of that part of the Church in which I live, my community. Today, after two thousand years, we have to ask what can replace immediate contact or meeting with Christ? It is contact or relations with witnesses who have identified their existence with him, those in whom he has grown interiorly so that his life is part of theirs. This experience of what we are calling a transparence is to be shared among human beings; it is a meeting of souls where God is revealed. This is what St. John says in his first Epistle: "That which we have seen, that we have watched and touched with our hands: the Word who is life—this is what we announce to you" (1 Jn. 1). Here, as in the Gospel, the commandment to love one another is not only a moral, ethical order, as a means of obeying a Prophet, of imitating him; but it is the very place, the means of a revealing meeting. The meeting with Jesus can be shared in interpersonal dialogue and relations, and so is carried on the initial meeting of the early witnesses. Not only do we believe, hope and love what they believed, hoped and loved, but we share what we believe, hope and love, what we have and what we are.

How can this mediating interpersonal relation become a historical-cultural one in our social milieu? . . . This can be accomplished by and in the Church, by the mediation of Community in and with Christ: the Church which exists historically with its language, its culture, but always in continuity with the founding language which guarantees this immediate and community mediation among those who have received and accepted the manifestation of God. Community dialogue is made possible by what the Bible and Tradition call the Spirit—as Spirit immanent in God Three Persons, as Mediator—He who gives, who sends, who shares the history, the event of salvation.

Under what forms do we find this mediation of the Church? First there is the word of God written and

preached; then the profession of faith of the Church which
gives coherence to all these elements in Scripture and
Tradition; then the community of the Church which is
both the fundamental community of life and milieu from
which each one receives this manifestation by faith, and
the universal community with her authority, sacraments
and rites. No one of these means must make us forget the
others. These are the means by which we receive the
manifestation of God that was in Christ, for himself in
his experience and for the witnesses in their paschal experience. Such are the means by which we can participate in
this experience, pass it on, share it and communicate it.
This, of course, is true for all Christians, but particularly so
for contemplatives whose life is exemplary Christian life
because it is exclusive. Since the Word in Christ is the
principle of light for every man coming into this world,
because this Word is the way, the truth and the life,
whenever I participate in him, I do so in the name of every
man as every man does. With every human being I share
the way of salvation, truth and life. If I failed to do so,
would he be deprived of such participation? No, he would
not. But I *want* this participation, I consent to it, I am united
to it and in this sense, I consciously contribute to it. Jesus is
the way that I follow and it is good for me to know this. I do
nothing alone and it is important that the transparence of
Jesus in me be apparent to others. How can this be? Here
we enter into the realm of the practical. There are several
ways of making this transparence evident, of witnessing to
it, and each one of us, each group, each institution must
find ways. First, however, we must be convinced that a
certain sharing of this transparence is part of our vocation.
Jesus alone saves, but when I love God in him, the love of
God shows in me. We can be united to the transparence of
God in Jesus Christ by proclaiming or making known the
Word he has given to men; by imitating him in our actions,
he who did all things well; but also by manifesting his

prayer: prayer in which he experienced and will experience eternally, the presence of God within him. Such witness supposes for some people the renouncement of other forms of transparence; it is a vocation in the Church. It is not the only one but the Church accepts it, assuring us that it has a meaning because it is one way of making God transparent to men.

We must keep our confidence alive. We must maintain our faith in our vocation, our hope for ourselves and for the Church at this time when she sees the breaking up of familiar socio-cultural structures to which she once contributed and on which she relied to some extent. The Church is being born again according to the Gospel without any other support than the Holy Spirit, there where all cultural support tends to disappear. Today and tomorrow we find ourselves at bay, obliged to live the experience of the Resurrection, to *believe*, despite what sometimes seems to us to be a sort of death of the Church, and what is in fact, a death of Christian cultures. We are up against a situation where we can expect from the Church no other transparence than that of the death and resurrection of Jesus. Witness of faith in Jesus and nothing else. Whatever else there may be will be given over and above and will not be lacking. But the Church must first pass through—as she is doing—this purification which John Paul II defines when he distinguishes between the domain of the Church and the domain of secular societies. It is amidst all these considerations that we must situate a theology of our contemplative life and its role in the Church.

CHRIST AND THE PRIMITIVE MONASTIC IDEAL

Jean Gribomont, OSB
*(Monk of the Abbey of
Clervaux, Luxembourg and
of St. Jerome's Abbey, Rome)*

"Who do you say that I am?" (Mt. 16:15)

The question is only asked once in the Gospel—at the climax of the Apostles' formation. The fascinating discovery of Jesus' personality ("Come and see," Jn. 2:39), the abandonment of all in order to follow him (*passim*) and the revelation of his unique relationship with the Father mark the stages of ascent to that faith in him of which salvation consists. Even the apparently less personal teaching directed to the crowds is always at least implicitly intended to draw them to him. The Beatitudes proclaim his coming: "Blessed are you. . ." because *I have come* to overthrow the privilege of the oppressors, the rich and the powerful, and to establish the kingdom of God. The parables illustrate the paradoxes of this kingdom: but who is the Bridegroom, the master of the household, the judge of the last day? Long before being able to "say who I am," Jesus' hearers, the crowds who see him driving out demons, are forced to come to some conclusion, ill-defined but impressive, about the Son of Mary, and in the light of that to reconsider their ideas about the law, righteousness, truth, their neighbor, themselves and about the Father.

When the apostolic preaching reached more distant societies, the Gospel was still always Jesus, and Jesus crucified (1 Cor. 1:23). The most searching analysis of the New Testament is constantly uncovering the prophetic models which were used as vehicles to put across salvation history, the Suffering Servant, the Son of Man, the Son of David.

To what extent does this central point which flavors the whole New Testament remain the key to the whole of the Church's teaching? This is the first question that a Christian reading of the history of dogma raises, whether we take as our point of departure the history of exegesis, catechesis or spirituality. The answer is not to be found in a standard formula, but rather diffused through the lives and experiences of the saints (as already in the lives of the apostles), with the result that in verbal and conceptual terms its expression remains incomplete, or else is expressed as a reaction counter to whatever system of human wisdom was the current cause of concern. Hence some sort of "philology," the ability to make a levelheaded interpretation of the historical background, is necessary for a true understanding. The result of an insufficiently critical reading of the texts is a so-called "edifying" hagiographical perspective, insipid, lacking seasoning or bite. The opposite error claims to find in the saints and doctors of the Church people who are heretics, revolutionaries or unbalanced. There is a truth in this, but their exaggerations were at the service of the growth of the faith, as agents of change and development.

We would like here to cast an eye over the origins of monastic institutions in the Eastern Church of the fourth and fifth centuries. There we find a whole body of literature, basic works which are spiritual classics even in the West (the "Life of Antony," the "Sayings of the Fathers," St. Basil, some of Jerome's letters, Cassian) and others less well-known, because they were less in tune with the later development of monasticism, and which are often recent discoveries in such languages as Coptic, Syriac, Armenian and Ethiopian. These open up to us the classic texts, and often bring out the complex, gnostic and combative characters of real Christianity and monasticism, which found its niche in the Churches through internecine struggles and conflicts with the powers of culture, the State and the Church hierarchy. Let us take the example of Origen, of the Origenist heritage (the Letters of Antony, the Treatises of Evagrius), and, further to the "left," the gnostic Coptic library rediscovered at Nag Hammadi. Of course, all these texts resurrect the question of how we should understand the standard classics themselves. Furthermore, besides the literary evidence, there is all we now know of economic and social life, with its stresses and interrelationships with cultural development. For example, Professor G. Dagron's remarkable study, *Naissance d'une capitale* (Paris, 1974), now allows us to understand the origins, which the accounts which have come down to us had intentionally obscured, of the monastic movement in Constantinople. It is with this more precise approach that we propose to assess the witness to Jesus.

We well know what a struggle the bishops and theologians had, using the terminology of Greek thought, to formulate the mystery of Christ in official credal statements, a mystery continually put before the community by Scripture and tradition, especially the liturgical tradition of the sacraments. However great the genius of the believer, e.g., that of Origen, and however great the quality of their contribution to the growth of Christian thought, it could never simultaneously encompass every aspect of divine truth. The very fact that a given presentation of that truth suited a given era and culture entailed its unsuitability for another period or place—and this quite apart from the fact that the stature of the disciple or interpreter was not always on a par with the master; that too often that intellectual fellow-feeling which is born of charity and is an indispensable condition for brotherly understanding was stifled by conflicts of ecclesiastical political interest.

The chief obstacle to a right development of Christology (and of soteriology, which is almost identical to it) was a rationalist tendency to reduce the divine mystery to what the highest philosophies had been able to understand of it. After docetism, which reduced the human reality of God the Savior, came, during the fourth century, a series of forms of Arianism, which subordinated God the Word, incarnate, to the Father, the only God in the strict sense. Then, in the fifth century (and after), within the frame of the Trinitarian faith, a wide variety of Christologies explained the personal unity and the divine and human duality of the incarnate Christ in differing fashions. Some very worthy Churches which are still today separated from the Byzantine and Roman communion, maintain these divisions, in Egypt, Syria, Ethiopia or elsewhere. In their heyday they formed perhaps the larger and more committed part of Christendom, and only the uninformed reckon that mere silliness and childishness brought about such divisions. For believers, it was a matter of confessing their faith in the divinity of the Savior. There is no doubt that the too purely-human view of the figure of Christ which many Westerners have would gain from being enlivened by the veneration and devotion of the pre-Chalcedonian Churches. But whatever might be the gains, and at any rate the legitimacy, of a true theological pluralism and of ecumenical respect for the great traditions of the Christian East, the best historians of these conflicts now recognize the misunderstandings which caused the reciprocal anathemas, the hunger for power which distorted the parts played by the great apostolic sees of Alexandria and Rome, by Byzantium, too, and by others. The Pontiffs who occupy these sees today have all expressed their sorrow for the deeds of the past and sought to overcome bitterness by humility and hospitality in charity. The actions of these Church leaders obviously imply some sort of contribution from the generality of Christians to the recovery of the fullness of the confession of the Lord Christ, going beyond the insular self-sufficiency and

pharisaical complacency which as unconsciously contami-
nate the Westerners of the twentieth century as they did
the Easterners of ancient times. Would it not be an inex-
pressible joy to learn the "length, the breadth and the
depth" of the mystery of Christ from the apostolic tradition handed down by the Twelve accounts?

Our concern here is, what is the link between these
eastern Christological developments and the flowering of
monastic life, so characteristic of these same Eastern
Churches of Egypt, Syria and Palestine, at the very time of
the Nestorian and Monophysite crises, or, more strictly
speaking, just before (Ephesus, 431, marks the eruption of
these crises) the anti-Arian century during which the
future misunderstandings were brewing? Admittedly,
even one who has spent years studying these languages,
these complex developments and their varied spiritual
progeny is forced to admit the limits of his knowledge. I am
at present preparing a course for use this year in the
Gregorian University on this subject, and can see that it
will be quite difficult to lead even a select group of well-
prepared students through this maze. So, in default of
being able to discuss the texts and set out their underlying
ideas here, I hope simply to arouse the reader's curiosity,
and to help him to form an overall picture.

Let us say at the outset, that very fortunately, the
monks in general refrained from embroiling themselves in
theological polemic. They had understood clearly that faith
in Christ, or in the action of the Spirit, or in the creative
and redemptive plan of the Father is far from being the
same as human wisdom and systematic theological and
philosophic exactitude. We must avoid making them out to
be holier and wiser than they were; at times they put in
an appearance on the battlefield—the streets of the cities
or the aisles of the churches—to support by bawling or
brawling what they believed to be the orthodox teaching,
even against doctors, bishops and armies. We could draw

up long lists of the heroic deeds of their monastic resistance, actions of differing merit by holy monks resisting the powers backing up the confession of faith in question. While deprecating their blind obstinacy, perhaps the historian should still respect their generous sacrifice of personal interest, and might express the wish that governments and bishops renounce the use of force to smother debate.

The Sayings of the Fathers

Be that as it may, the most authoritative monastic tradition is careful to avoid setting up the spiritual fathers as judges, or to involve them in the niceties of debate. It unconcernedly distinguishes the act of religious faith from all intellectual explanations. Here is one of the oldest and most authoritative texts (Antony, Apophthegm 17, which has solid backing in the alphabetic and systematic collections):

> Some old men came one day to Abba Antony, and Abba Joseph was with them. *Wishing to try them,* the old man put to them a saying from Scripture, and, starting with the youngest, asked them the meaning of the saying; and each did his best to explain it. But the old man said to each: "You have not yet found out what it means." Lastly, he said to Abba Joseph: "You, how do you interpret this word?" He answered: "I do not know." Then Abba Antony said: "Truly, Abba Joseph has found out how, by saying, 'I do not know.' "

We should not interpret this saying as a condemnation of the exegetical Gospel homily, still less as a craven refusal to understand the word of God. Such an attitude would not only be contradicted by abundant contrary evidence, but would be contrary to the continual "meditatio," rumination of the word of God, which is the basic element in monastic prayer. What is condemned is not use of the intellect, but "empty curiosity," a radical divergence from humbly chewing over the biblical food.

We may well regret that these worthy hermits should have feared literal and historical study of the Bible; doubtless they risked suffering in their spiritual health from the vitamin deficiency of their diet. However, let us note in passing, that their lack of literary culture left them no choice in this matter; they had enough common sense to see the unacceptable risks that unskilled use of the tools of scientific criticism could pose for those of weaker understanding. Furthermore, this did not constrain the likes of Basil, Jerome, Didymus and Evagrius from offering the Church, via their use of these tools, their own bold and often enduring contributions. Their chief preoccupation was with a moral interpretation, proven by its fruits and its conformity with the example of the Fathers. What was, on the contrary condemned by (almost) all, including those such as Basil and Jerome and the orthodox doctors in general, was venturesome speculation and all philosophical interpretation of the part played by Christ. For the rest, what is praised in Abba Joseph is his genuine humility and his preference for listening rather than speaking. We may even meet these qualities in a preacher!

It must be admitted that the "Sayings of the Fathers" rarely mention Christ's name (see the invaluable index compiled by the monks of Solesmes in *Les Sentences des Pères du Désert*, III, 1976, p. 338, s.v. "Christ"). However, I would point out a significant, though less well attested text, Poemen 144:

> Abba Joseph (not the same as the one mentioned earlier) told of Abba Isaac's having said this: One day as I was sitting by Abba Poemen, I saw him go into ecstasy. As I was on very close terms with him, I made a prostration to him, and asked, "Tell me, where were you?" He was embarrassed and said to me, "My thoughts were there where holy Mary, the mother of God, was standing weeping beside the cross of the Savior [Jn. 19:25]; I wish I could weep like that always."

Despite the silence of the early Latin version, the chain

of transmission through Isaac and Joseph leaves one favorably convinced of its historicity.

The rarity of Gospel quotations in the collections of "Sayings" should come as no surprise to us, for of those collected, only the short and pithy, intentionally "practical" were retained. Besides, the collection was gathered together after Archbishop Theophilos had purged the Egyptian hermitages of a whole Origenist tradition, and monks were not the only ones to suffer expulsion, it is equally certain that a fair chunk of the "Sayings" fell victim to the same fate.

The Letters of St. Antony

If it is thought that this source's concern with moral and eremitical questions, rather than being, in Augustine Roberts' fine phrase defining monastic life, "centered on Christ" (St. Bede's Publications, 1979), is exceptional, then it is worthwhile to go back to a much older and unquestionably authentic document, The Letters of Antony (which I quote in the order of the Georgian version, in André Louf's edition, published at Bellefontaine as number 19 of the *Spiritualité Orientale* collection in 1976). There is much that is quotable, but we shall have to limit ourselves to a page.

Antony sees Christian and monastic life as a continuation of God's interventions and covenants, of which the Incarnation is the peak. The goal is to return to the primordial Unity of the image of God with its creator.

> We know God did not visit his creatures once only. From the beginning of the world, those who found the way to their Creator in the law of the Covenant [Antony seems to have in mind Adam, Noah, Abraham] have all had the company of his goodness, his grace and his Spirit. In his untiring love, the Creator of all things sought to visit us in our afflictions and dissipation: he raised up Moses the lawgiver who gave us the written law and laid the foundations of the House of truth,

the Catholic Church. He did not complete it, he left it and passed on. Then came the band of Prophets raised up by the Spirit of God. They too carried on the building on Moses' foundation, without being able to finish it. Each recognized that the wound was incurable and that no creature could heal it, save the only Son, faithful image of the Father, the image of him who created beings endowed with reason in that image. So they came together and presented to God a unanimous prayer on behalf of the members of that family of which we are part.

Therefore God, overflowing with love, came to us, saying through the voice of his saints: "Son of man, prepare for yourself an exile's baggage" (Ez. 12:3). And he, the image of God (2 Cor. 4:4) did not count equality with God a thing to be grasped, but humbled himself, taking the form of a servant, he became obedient unto death, even death on a cross. Therefore God has bestowed on him the Name which is above every name, that at the Name of Jesus Christ every knee should bow (Phil. 2:6-10). Now that saying has been fulfilled among you: "To save us the love of the Father did not spare his only Son but gave him up for our salvation on account of our sins" (Rm. 8:32). Our iniquities were his humiliations, his wounds made us whole (Is. 53:5). His all-powerful Word has gathered us together from every nation, from the earth's ends, from the farthest bounds of the universe, raising up our souls, forgiving our sins, teaching us that we are one another's members.

I beg you, brothers, by the name of our Lord Jesus Christ, enter into that marvelous Economy of salvation: "He was made like to us in all things but sin" (Heb. 4:15). Every being endowed with spiritual understanding—for each of whom the Lord came—must take stock of his own nature, in other words he must know himself and use discernment to distinguish good from evil, if he wishes to find freedom at the coming of the Lord. They already bear the name of *servants* of God, who have gained their freedom through that Economy of salvation. But the final goal is not there; this is only the righteousness of this present hour, this is only the way to filial adoption. Jesus, our Savior, who knew that they had received the Spirit of sonship and that it was thanks to the teaching of the Holy Spirit that they knew him, said to them: "No longer shall I call you servants, but *brothers* and friends" (Jn. 15:15). Their spirit was emboldened: they knew him thenceforward with their spiritual nature; and they cried out: "Up to now we used to know you in your body, but thus no longer" (2 Cor. 5:16). They received the Spirit which made them adoptive sons, and they proclaimed: "The Spirit which we have received is no longer a spirit which enslaves and leads back to earth, but a Spirit which makes us adoptive sons...heirs of God and fellow-heirs with Christ" (Rm. 8:17). (Ep. 2, 1-4; ed. Louf, pp. 51-54).

Antony doesn't always manage to fly quite so high, nor to express himself so clearly, but his letters are full of parallels, returning to this speculation, this gnosis, one might say, using this Greek loan-word with its Biblical and Alexandrian meaning. Through the covenants, the laws, the prophets, he follows the road towards the humiliation and the cross of the only Son, the perfect image of the immortality of the Father and transcendent model of the spiritual nature created by him. Monastic life is simply the reply to that love, not just in servile fashion, but as sons vivified by the Spirit of Christ. The emphasis placed, in passing, on knowledge of our own "spiritual nature," accompanied by discernment of good and evil, should not be condemned as heretical, even if it betrays to us a strong Origenist influence (which appears the more pronounced if one reads the whole of Antony).

I lack space here for detailed comment on this passage, so I would rather just suggest you reread it. It is certainly on another plane from the "Sayings of the Fathers," and if it antedates them, we are forced to admit that anti-Origenist circles allowed this collection of letters to be lost, if they did not deliberately suppress it.

St. Pachomius

There exists plentiful literary material, associated

with the figure of Pachomius in the south of Egypt, of considerable historical and intellectual worth, on the origins of the *koinonia* (community) or cenobitic life. Unfortunately, it is difficult to be sure that a written tradition goes back to Pachomius himself, save in the case of a few obscure and peculiar letters. His disciples and successors, Horsiesius and Theodore, were the ones who recorded him for posterity and appointed themselves as his apostles and evangelists.

The Pachomian ideal of purity of heart is very close to that of the hermits of Scete, but consciously bases itself on Mt. 5:8 (which is thrice quoted in the authoritative Coptic "Life"). Quotations of the words of Jesus, or of Paul on more strictly Christian matters, occur quite naturally in the explanations of the Saint and his disciples, and visibly guide their lifestyle. The preface to the "Life," common to the Greek and Coptic texts (even if the first page of this latter has been accidentally lost to us) develops a theme curiously akin to what we read in Antony, the theme of the word of God to Abraham, to Moses, to the prophets, and finally of the concluding blessing bestowed by this Word when he commissioned his Apostles, in Mt. 28:19. Clearly, in the author's view, baptism and monastic vocation are identified, at least in Pachomius' case. The prologue fits the mention of the martyrs into its outline history, and these lead on to the appearance of the monasteries, to Antony and to the Father of the *koinonia*.

While the importance of Christ in these circles is unquestionable, one may ask to what extent this Christ is truly distinct from God. Not that one would suggest that Pachomius might have been some sort of Sabellian, denying the Trinity; he is inarguably at St. Athanasius' side in his defense of orthodoxy. But Christ is always seen as united with the Father and as his mouthpiece. When the lively imagination of the Saint expresses itself in (splendid) visions on the east wall of the sanctuary, the Lord who appears is (Bohairic Life, 73) simultaneously God and Christ, to whom one can cry: "Have mercy on me, my Lord Jesus Christ." There is nothing heterodox about this, but it is perhaps the playing-down of the part played by Christ as mediator which leaves so much scope for angelic interventions, which are so typical of these accounts.

One of the authentic documents we have, is a catechesis by Theodore. He relies on the teaching and example of the founder, but not without linking it closely to the Lord by way of the apostles. For example (ed. L. Th. Lefort, *Oeuvres de S. Pachôme et de ses Successeurs*, Louvain, 1964, French text, p. 43): "In trouble, let us say . . . : 'Who shall separate us from the love of God?' (Rm. 8:35). Just as the Apostle acted, the chosen one of God, who said to us: 'Be imitators of me, as I am of Christ' (1 Cor. 11:1). Those who have worthily finished their contest, and have found rest from their labors by entering the place of their eternal rest, all the saints and all the fathers of the *koinonia* also did likewise." Clearly then, the figure of the Saint plays a central part in the rule proposed for the brethren, but this comes about through his apostolic imitation of the only definitive model. The theory is open to argument, but raises no difficulties for Coptic orthodoxy.

Further on (on the same page) the theme crops up again: "Holding fast to the end by the strength *of Christ*, happy to suffer infirmities, insults, anguish, persecutions and troubles *for Christ*, we shall truly inherit all the blessings of the Scriptures, breath of God, and the promises made to our fathers; not only we, but whoever has loved the holy life of the *koinonia*; has shared the humiliation *of Christ* . . . as the Apostle says: 'All who desire to live a godly life *in Christ Jesus* will also be persecuted' (2 Tm. 3:12)." Once again, a strict cenobitic observance is seen in the light of the example and strength of Christ, in a Pauline tradition.

From another point of view, the sacrament which unites us to Christ, and the resurrection of which it is the guarantee, explains monastic chastity and the sanctification of the body itself:

> Who does not know the sweetness of purity, the assurance it gives before God and men, at the moment of approaching the holy altar and the body and blood of the Lord? Could anyone ...have the least wish for damnable impurity, when he dwells on the day of the resurrection by which the Lord 'will change our lowly body to be like his glorious body' (Phil. 3:21)? Or again, he who has experienced the simplicity of a pure heart; who has cast himself on the Lord's breast (cf. Jn. 13:23) in the joy of a heart free from faults... (p. 44).

That the allusion to the Last Supper and to John's intimacy with his master should follow mention of the Eucharist so closely is worthy of note; one would bet, from the context of chastity from which he writes, that Theodore would approach the sacrament with bold and tender devotion.

Monastic discipline aims at being evangelical, and obedience relies on Revelation for its basis: "By *listening* we make ourselves Jesus' servants (cf. Eph. 6:6), as we know from having heard the voice of the Father declaring in the Gospels: 'This is my beloved son, in whom I am well pleased; *listen to him*' " (p. 52).

Theodore has fine things to say about the founding fathers of the community, whom death has removed from the scene: "Which of the faithful would ever proclaim: Paul, or Apollos or Cephas saves me? We have all heard the Lord say to his chosen disciples: 'If you loved me, you would rejoice because I go to my Father, for my Father is greater than I' (Jn. 14:28)? And again: 'If I go away, the Paraclete shall come to you' (Jn. 15:26)" (p. 55). It is a fine thing that the Gospel of Christ, having been the basis of Pachomius' authority and example, should also be the means of transcending the limits imposed by his earthly life.

St. Basil

His brother, Gregory of Nyssa, and his close friend, Gregory Nazianzen, form the setting for St. Basil. To his thorough Athenian cultural formation, and his outstanding feeling for the responsibilities of government and of the Church he added attentive study of what was his first priority, the New Testament, especially the Gospel. He achieved this synthesis because after his humanist formation he broke with his brilliant career and his social class, to become a part of the monastic movement (with a visit to Syria and to Egypt), and more particularly of the "revolutionary" groups of Asia Minor influenced by Eustathius of Sebaste. While we are on the subject, it is worth remarking on the fact that women played a part both noteworthy and criticized in these groups; Basil's mother and sister had preceded him and undoubtedly influenced his course.

It has often been pointed out that the ancient wisdom of the Platonists and the Stoics played an important part in the Basilian synthesis; one finds their ideals and balance everywhere. These are conscious borrowings, fully proportioned to and knitted into what is strictly in harmony with Scripture, rather than (though this had, however, its own truth and importance) precisely what the Constantinian Church was prepared to sanction. At the beginning of his "conversion," alerted by the squabbles and excesses which were apparent to right and left, as equally among the ascetics as among the bishops (and Basil has no qualms about criticizing them, individually and in the mass) the Saint devoted years to coming to know the scriptural standard in all its details, with the words of Jesus as the norm. Whenever he speaks out later on, we can be sure that before speaking, his enlightened gaze has picked out whichever Gospel precepts are applicable, and to which he must lead his hearers. Depending on circumstances, the quotation may be set out at the very beginning of the explanation, or it may be introduced by a rhetorical and

sapiential build-up; but it is the quotation which is normative. One cannot over-emphasize the fact that the word of
Christ is definitive and sets the tone of the whole discourse. The powerful "mystique," with its zeal for poverty,
virginity, prayer and complete purity of heart, which was
the driving force of the Eustathian groups, is, if one can use
such language, brutally sacrificed to it, a clear case of
pruning the vine so that it may bear more fruit.

In numerous individual studies I have come to recognize
this ordered structure, which I limit myself to recalling
here. In my opinion, probably a trifle biased, Basil's friends,
and especially Gregory of Nyssa (who published scarcely
anything until after his brother's death) reaped the fruits
of the harvest that he had energetically prepared for them
—and for many others.

Even so, one would expect such an eminent thinker, so
strongly Christ-centered, to make a quite special contribution to reflection on the Mystery of the Incarnation. But
historians of this doctrine have hardly anything to say
about his contribution.

In point of fact, naturally enough, they devote their
attention to the problems which, revolving around the
persons and teachings of Nestorius and Cyril of Alexandria, were to divide the Churches at Ephesus and at Chalcedon. The development of Christology is conventionally
seen in terms of the disputes caused by Apollinarius, about
the *nous* of Christ; then of the repercussions of these disputes in Antiochene circles, with their affirmation of a
perfect human nature, subject to natural growth, and the
historical exegesis of the Gospels and of Paul; then of the
Alexandrian insistence on the complementary truth, the
one incarnate and saving divine nature. In vain does one
seek in Basil signs of any conflict between these two view-
points. He uses some Alexandrian formulae, others of
Antiochene provenance, and not only seems unaware of
any contradiction between them, but also refuses to

involve himself or to take it seriously when Epiphanius of
Salamis draws his attention to the dawning conflict (Letter
258, 2). With perfect courtesy, albeit not without gentle
raillery, he congratulates Epiphanius on his concern for
orthodoxy and his conciliatory spirit (!), and explains his
own irenic rejoinder, which is to put in a demurrer to these
denunciations:

> I have always admired your pain at the squabbles of the
> brethren of the Mount of Olives, and your efforts to restore
> peace among them.... We have already replied to our dearly
> beloved brothers of the Mount of Olives.... We said we
> could add nothing to the profession of faith of Nicaea, not
> even one little word.... As for the doctrines on the Incarna-
> tion of the Lord with which people are embroidering that
> faith, we have neither examined them nor accepted them, as
> being matters too deep for our understanding. We are well
> aware that as soon as we abandon the *simplicity of the faith* there
> will be no limit to our discussion, because it will lead us on
> further; and we will disturb simple souls by the fruitless
> introduction of matters extraneous to the faith.

What a prophetic insight into the quarrels which were to
divide the Churches for centuries, resulting in the Christians' weakness in the face of the Persians and then of
Islam, and also the separation of the West from Constantinople, despite apparent agreement at the Council of
Chalcedon! If only the theologians of the great Sees of the
fifth century, Nestorius and his opponents, could have had
the same breadth of vision, the same civilization of
approach, the same faith!

It is no surprise, in these circumstances, that Basil's
speculation provides no fuel for the coming controversies
about the two natures; this is neither ignorance nor in-
difference, but rather an intentional abreaction, and his
piercing and balanced assessment of the various influences
already at work is at least as faithful a reflection of the true
Church tradition as a fulmination of anathemas aimed in

every direction. Historians, then, should not seek in Basil to find implicit condemnations of the future Nestorians and Monophysites, but how he blends and balances the positive contributions of both. True enough, this is the product of his intellectual genius; but equally it is the product of his deliberate choice in favor of Gospel values, and, if you like, of monasticism.

In the first issue of *Word and Spirit* (1979, pp. 109-130) I showed this intellectual taciturnity of Basil's combining "Intrasigence and Irenicism" in the matter of the proclamation of the Holy Spirit. The Saint would not dream of hiding the truth, of putting the proclamation (the *kerygma*) of salvation brought by the Son and the Spirit under a bushel. What makes him more restrained than less enlightened theologians is the fact that he is more conscious of the relative character, *foreign* to the New Testament (see the last word of paragraph two, quoted above of Letter 258—*tèi pareisagôgèi tôn xenizontôn*), of the matters under discussion. He knew very well that all around him Apollinarius was being condemned for denying the existence in Christ of a human *nous*; but he was wary of taking up a position on this speculative ground, foreign in fact to the language and problematic of the Gospels, and on to which, furthermore, Apollinarius himself only ventured reluctantly, and when forced to do so. Without naming Apollinarius, Basil opposes his errors, but only in his analysis of the passions of Christ, which is important for the spiritual life, because in this area the Lord is an admirable model. Basil insists on the full and free acceptance of the natural passions, such as hunger and suffering; for him, the absolute rejection of any sinful or disordered element in the passions is entirely harmonious with this subjection to the human condition, for his understanding of man free and without sin is (almost too) clear. On the day when historians of Christology are prepared to dwell on this side of things in the teaching of the Cappadocians, then per-

haps will their eyes be opened to the richer eastern tradition, and they will be able to take the measure of the
deviations which misunderstandings of the different con-
ceptions of the person and the natures have led to.

To some extent, then, Basilian theology surprisingly
links up with popular Egyptian monastic theology, in its
sober reserve and respect for the mystery. However fleeting and superficial may have been the sketch presented
here, it may lead perhaps to a new understanding of the
texts, disencumbered from questionings that are out of
place, attentive more to the spiritual content than to the
development—intentionally omitted—of the terms over
which the arguments would rage.

Monasticism as a Whole

We have only been able to touch on a few examples, far
too few to form the basis of a synthesis.

In 1964, Uta Ranke-Heinemann, aided and abetted by
the advanced state of German scholarship, put forward
in a well-considered volume, *Das frühe Mönchtum*, the
fundamental themes of primitive monasticism, according
to its own self-testimony (Hans Driewer Verlag, Essen).
The limits of the work (143 small pages) and its synthetic
character do not allow it to distinguish either different
associations of people or epochs: it is more a doctrinal than
a strictly historical study. In fact, one even feels the need to
sound a cautionary note against the author's method,
which is purposely based on the witness given by the
monastic sources to the well-springs of the movement. In
fact these sources tend to overplay the Christian and
evangelical character of the saints they celebrate; given the
hypothetical case of a more-or-less gnostic or schismatic
group, would it not obviously be inclined to describe itself
(for internal consumption at first) as being animated by
edifying and supernatural motives? And this does not even
make allowance for the fact that the surviving texts which

succeeding generations received and broadcast are those
which bear the seal of doctrinal orthodoxy!

Let us be clear then, that the testimony adduced by Mrs.
Ranke-Heinemann presents a slightly rosier view than the
reality; her synthesis is nonetheless richly documented for
all that, and can stand our investigation in good stead. Her
account is divided into eight chapters, of which each of the
first six is devoted to one motivating idea:

I.   The love of God.
II. Expectation of death and the Parousia.
III. The drive for perfection.
IV. The struggle against the demons and sin.
V.   The angelic life.
VI. To follow Christ.

The last two chapters study the relationships between
primitive monasticism and the Church and the world.

We could draw out the influence of Christology in each
of these eight chapters. Even if love of God, the drive for
perfection, the (utopian?) hankering for a purely spiritual,
angelic life, freed from the flesh are themes found in every
religion and in a fair number of philosophies, it can scarcely
be denied that we also read of them in the Gospel and the
Epistles, and that is where, thanks to the sovereign power
of Jesus, most monks have discovered their power of
attraction.

However, let us devote our attention to the expectation
of the Kingdom of God, so fundamental to the primitive
Gospel, and the call to follow Christ.

As we run our eye over the list of texts she has used, we
must first of all point out that the author has not tried to
get back to strictly primitive monastic texts. She quotes
some highly interesting texts, such as the Syrian Aphra-
ates, a witness to a non-Mediterranean ascetical Christianity, but not strictly monastic. Rather, most of the texts laid
before us are those of a second, interpretative stage, like

the Life of Antony, but written after the death of the hero by a great bishop, for a wider public and with the object of putting across an interpretation of his life that will be helpful to the Church.

Chapter II shows that expectation of the Parousia is most often seen as a preparation for death. There remains an element of disillusionment with fleeting earthly life, but the Messianic vigil recedes into the background. That is more or less the conclusion we came to in reading the "Sayings of the Fathers." Let us beware of misjudging the Christian character of this "rejection of the world" and of this hope; equally, we should recognize that it is not the only thing that matters.

Chapter VI (one would be curious to know what led the author to arrange her subject matter in this order) is the one which has most bearing on our subject; it is backed up by ninety-six notes, and not a few quote several witnesses. It would certainly present no difficulty to enrich the collection still further. The author has highlighted allusions to Christ *crucified*, self-abnegation involving dying to the world, meaning (as a minimum) abandoning family and property, but with the intention of preparing for the spiritual sacrifice of self, through which one discovers a higher life in Christ. It is a baptismal theme, which rules the life of every Christian. Without wishing to insist that every monk express himself in terms of this vocabulary, it would be profitable to analyze and compare the largest possible number of texts from this stance, which would amount, in the end, to the compilation of a history of the monastic exegesis of Mt. 19:21 and 29 and 10:37 (and their parallels).

As is well known, from generation to generation the quintessential eastern monastic prayer has been cast in the form: "Lord Jesus, son of the living God—Have mercy on me, a sinner." The aspiration of the first part should constantly gain depth of meaning in the consciousness of the dialogue between the Jesus of the Gospel, of the sacraments and of the Church, and the Father whose image he is. The second part, repeated as each breath is expelled, presupposes that this Absolute of glory has come as Savior of the humble and the unworthy. The more I know myself to be a sinner, the better I know myself (and not, as in the letter of Antony, in my immortal spiritual nature!), and the more his mercy bears me up and renews me.

Certainly, such a relationship with him who revealed the Beatitudes and the Kingdom of God, with the Crucified, with the Risen, with him who is present in the sacraments and to the ascetic in his solitude, is no invitation to the dialectical antics of doctrinal controversy. It leads us, rather, as it led Antony, as it led Poemen, as it led Basil, to the knowledge of Christ, the knowledge that was Paul's, the knowledge of the Christ of the Apocalypse, the knowledge of Christ of the first or of the fourth Gospel.

Translated from the French by Giles Conacher, OSB, of Pluscarden Abbey, Scotland.

CHRIST IN THE RULE OF ST. BENEDICT

Martin Cawley, OCSO

*(Monk of Guadalupe Abbey,
Lafayette, Oregon)*

Like my previous article (*Word & Spirit* 2, pp. 82-110), this present one is mainly philological in nature and popular in style, being derived not from a wide acquaintance with periodical literature but from study of the concordances and being prepared not for publication but for simple talks to my community. It owes a particular debt to the encouragement and suggestions of Fr. John Baptist Hasbrouck, our Prior, the popularizer in English of Dom Adalbert de Vogüé's works.

Apart from the Bible, references are almost entirely confined to the Rule of St. Benedict (RB), that of his predecessor, the Master (RM), and his life as written by St. Gregory the Great in the Second of his four Books of Dialogues (II Dial.).

Had this been a truly theological treatment, three issues would have had to be faced, which I have largely side-stepped: (i) how does one justify RB's virtual ignoring of the distinction of Christ from the Father? (ii) how does one justify his minimizing of mention of the Holy Spirit? and (iii) how does one justify his seeming lack of interest in the "historical" Christ? Awareness of these three questions has provoked in my mind the beginnings of answers, but space does not allow their inclusion here. Suffice it to say that, for RB, Christ is the vast reality of the whole economy *through* which we "go to God"; just as Paul, by metonymy names this economy "faith," Benedict names it "obedience," "participation in sufferings," "fellowship," "followership"...what we would call "fitting in." As for the Holy Spirit, there are beginnings of an answer in my previous article, in the sections on Personalism especially. As for the "Historical Christ," preparation of this article has taught me how Protestant a phenomenon has been the recent "search" under that name—not now *sola scriptura*, but *solus Jesus—reconstructus ab eruditis*, a far cry from the total Christ of the here and now!

More than half of this article is devoted to RB's ways of naming Christ. Deeply imbued with the courtesy of the sixth century, and yet partially transcending it in his concern to use "few and reasonable words," St. Benedict conveys a good deal of his notion of Christ simply by the care with which he alludes to him. There follows a second part in which I gather together the glimpses of Christ afforded by various perspectives or horizons which are orientated towards him; again, it is largely in terms of courtesy and honor as emerging in our own souls that we glimpse the Christ whom they envisage. A final section touches very briefly, not really on Christ as he is in himself, but at least on a more dynamic "Spectator" (to use a word St. Gergory highlights in II Dial.) and Providence. Vastly more could be said, but it is hoped that these few notes will enrich the reader's approach to the Rule; they would, in fact, be scarcely intelligible and of little use to any but a devotee of that venerable document.

I: How the Rule Names Christ

The names which RB uses for Christ take on added significance from the fact that St. Benedict's courtesy and reverence prompt him to a sparing use of any personal names and a significantly narrow range of personal titles. The two titles which seem to capsulize his Christology are "Lord" and "King"; the meaning of these will be clarified by examing their counterparts: "servanthood" and "soldiery."

a) Reverential Avoidance of the Divine Name

In our own pluralistic society, a devout layman will readily hide an allusion to God under such an expression as "it *was meant* to be" or "acting for *religious* motives." Similarly, such books of the OT as I Maccabees, written in a context of struggle for cultural survival, will develop circumlocutions for naming God, such as "help from *Heaven*" and the "invoking of *the Most High*." St. Benedict, in turn, being a man of "few and reasonable words," and wishing to avoid the blunt use of the *purum nomen*—what today might be called the "first-name basis"—is sparing of direct mention of the Divine Persons or even the Angels and the Devil. Instead he will use a title or an abstract noun or the personification of some aspect of God: *the Lord, the Divinity, the Divine Call....* Another such device in RB is the use of adjectives proper to God: *divine, dominical, evangelical...*, or shared between God and creatures: *holy, sacred, lovingkind....* Finally, this reverential circumlocution is achieved in RB by use of impersonal verbs, auxiliaries and passives, usually having an ethical and worshipful overtone, though these expressions can still be used in purely human contexts.

In regard to the use of titles in naming Christ, we would expect an analogy with the naming of senior monks: not the *purum nomen* but the name adorned with a title of foreign origin, *abbas* or *nonnus*, and so we are not surprised to find the Greek prayer *Kyrie eleison.* When the Rule names individual humans, it usually slips in an honorific title or adjective: Paul *the Apostle, holy* Jacob, *our holy Father* Basil...; in fact, even more often the personal name is omitted and only the title is given: *the Prophet, the Apostle, our Fathers....* It is not surprising that *the malignant Devil* can be named simply as *the Malignant.* The surprise is rather the rarity with which the names *Christ* and *God* are thus softened with the additive *the Lord*—uniquely in the expressions "the Lord Christ, the true King" and "the Lord God of the Universe" and a couple of biblical quotations. We will examine this phenomenon below. Less surprising is the

use of the abstract nouns, *the Divinity* and *the holy Trinity*, and
the personification of such realities as *the divine Voice, the
divine Call, the divine Scripture*—realities which can do such
personal things "saying, commanding, shouting, awaken-
ing from sleep, pointing out, inserting steps. . . ." Even the
Rule itself is personified; its Latin name being feminine, it
becomes a *"mistress* for all to follow."

Although RB uses the name *God* more than 100 times
and the title *the Lord* more than 50, recourse is often had to
the adjectives *divine* and *dominical* as substitutes. In such
standard and technical expressions as "the Work of God"
and "the Lord's Day," these adjectival substitutes are
hardly significant, but their accumulation has something
of a domestic ring about it, all the more charming for its
avoidance of familiarity: the *divine* law, voice, precepts,
utterance, reading, authority, task (*opus/officium*), tremor,
justice, grace, retribution. . .; the *dominical* day (Sunday),
prayer ("Our Father"), service, sheepfolds, precept. As for
other adjectives, their use is sparing but reverential and it
can flow over to qualify non-divine realities: *holy, sacred*
(*sacratus/sacer*), *loving-kind*. . .; the surprise is rather at the
absence of such superlatives as "most high, eternal,
almighty, heavenly" as direct epithets for God, especially
in the context of the vertical thrust and eternal dimension
of our own wayfaring in the Rule. "Heaven" does occur in
an adjectival, or rather an adverbial phrase with reference
to God, and the adverb *divinitus* is quite in place in RB, but
there seems to be more deliberation behind the adjectival
clauses which are coined to suit certain contexts and are
used without naming the Divine Person whom they qualify: "for the sake of him *who has loved us;* damned by him
whom he is mocking; to see him *who has called us. . . ."*

Modern letter writers often avoid beginning paragraphs
with the pronoun "I"; instead they will use such a passive
expression as "your letter has been received." Many passives in RB serve a similar purpose in avoiding the name of

God: "days *are relaxed* for us as an armistice...," "we *are discerned* in his sight...." Then there are those very Latin impersonal verbs, with a moral overtone and something of a divine horizon: *far be it; it is expedient...licit...opportune... decent...becoming.* The Latin of the sixth century abounded in what might be called "auxiliaries of courtesy": one did not say bluntly "Bless me, Sir," but "Give the command, Sir: 'Be thou blessed,' " alternatively translated as "Command, Sir, by way of blessing." These auxiliaries, *dignari, mereri, debere, jubere...*, abound in RM and in II Dial., but in RB they are much rarer and always functional. Thus "deigning" is used only of notable divine condescension by the Good Shepherd, "meriting" has definite eschatological overtones, and so on. There is a businesslike objectivity about this impersonality, a "fewness and reasonableness of words," which sets a tone of reverence against which to consider the more explicit names and titles of Christ.

b) The Range of Names and Titles for Christ in RB

Considerable light can be thrown on the Christology of RB by comparing the usage of the three terms, *God, Christ* and *the Lord.* Other, less frequent titles will also be considered.

We saw above that the names *God* and *Christ* had this in common, that each is normally used in RB as a *purum nomen,* where we would expect them to be softened by addition of the title *the Lord.* Furthermore, neither is ever qualified by an adjective or a possessive, with the one exception noted above: the Lord God *of the Universe.* On the other hand, both *God* and *Christ* are frequently used in expressions of love and honor, "love of God" and "love of Christ" being almost interchangeable. In fact the word *God* owes much of the great frequency of its use in RB to such possessive expressions or their equivalents in varied syntactical constructions; thus *God* is the recipient of "fear, honor, reverence," as well as of "love, dilection, charity," and recipient of "thanksgiving, accounting, duty (*opus/officium*), zeal, promise, offering, confession, lying, committing and exhibiting and applying of hope, obedience and credit," recipient also of "blessing and glorifying" as well as of "supplicating and asking. . . ." The term *God* is, in fact, an all-purpose term for religious contexts, and our over-all goal as monks is well expressed as a "seeking" of God, a "progressing" and a "going" along the way that "leads" to him. In the same way, but far less extensively, the term *Christ* can be used in such contexts, especially where "following" and "imitation" are involved. As for those transactions in which God is initiator rather than recipient, some are named in RB with the term *the Lord* as an alternative, but far more widely *God* is used: *God's* "grace, patience, mercy, retribution"; his "gift, aid, help, protection, shielding (*avertat*)"; his "kingdom and house"; his "sayings, commandments, precepts, judgment and sentence." Only in these last named is the term *the Lord* also used (apart from a couple of biblical quotations: the eyes, the Day of the Lord). Just one such instance is spontaneously used by RB, without precedent in RM; it regards a "precept" of Christ in the Gospel about fraternal correction. Thus the word *God* is an all-purpose term for transactions between a Divine Person and ourselves. In many instances it is comparable to the OT usage whereby "giant-sized" realities were called "the mountains of God, rivers of God, winds of God. . . ." This superlative sense can be illustrated conveniently from the use of the word *opus* (*opera*): a gradation exists in RB from the vituperated *opus peculiare* (private hoarding), through the neutral *opus suum* (one's own task) and the commendable *opera manuum* (manual work), to the lofty *opera bona* (good works) and finally to the giant-sized *opus divinum* or *opus Dei*. In such contexts the addition of a title to soften the name *God* would spoil the superlative effect. I suggest that the use of *Christ* as a *purum nomen* be understood along the same lines—"love of Christ," "holding nothing dearer than Christ," "receiving or listening to Christ"...would all be acts of superlative virtue, the loftiest love, the loftiest obedience—though not, of course with any loss of Christological reference. Reciprocally, what is "acceptable to God" is superlatively acceptable, unquestionably valid.

The terms *God* and *Christ*, thus used, have the syntactical form of proper names, if not the full logical criteria for such. RB never uses the personal name *Jesus*; in fact even the lengthier RM has it only three times, always in biblical or liturgical quotations. Yet there is an intimacy and an enthusiasm in the passages where RB uses the name *Christ*: three times it is a question of the "love" or "honor" to be shown to Christ; three times also of the "holding nothing dearer" or "preferable" to him; and then four times in the sense of receiving Christ in the sick or the guest, as we will see more fully in treating of lordship and servanthood.

As for the use of the term *the Lord*, it is quite frequent in the chapters shared by RM and RB, but after these it becomes notably less frequent and owes its inclusion mainly to biblical quotations. In several common passages, RB actually uses *God* in its place (in the tremendous judgment of *God*; render an account to *God* the most equitable judge...); such substitutions could have been made elsewhere too, for it is rarely demonstrable that *the Lord* meant is the Christ of the Gospels. However, when RB spontaneously uses the term in the later chapters, the addition of the adjectives "our" (RB 23:2 and 39:9) or "the one" (61:10) clearly has Christ in mind. The same is true of the "lovingkind" and the "dreadful" Lord spoken of in the Prologue (taken from RM). The same could be said of one other passage peculiar to RB and several in common, where the "Lord" of a quotation is the Christ of the Gospels (RB 64:21, etc.). However, there remain three more texts peculiar to RB, which throw important light on this "Lord" whom St. Benedict tends thus to qualify as "ours" (in each case it is the contemporary Lord, the Lord of Providence, who is in question, and the author who so readily uses reverential devices to avoid the divine name, hushes his little intimations of divine intervention behind this less usual term, "the Lord"): the guest who points out a local defect—"perhaps for this very thing it was that *the Lord* directed him here"; all are to be called to counsel—"for often it is to the junior that *the Lord* reveals what is best"; when all human means have failed with a delinquent, the abbot is to apply "what is greater, his own and all the brethren's prayer—that *the Lord*, who is capable of all things, might operate salvation upon the infirm brother." I find a charming little note of intimacy in the "perhaps" and the "often" and the "what is greater," along with the "who can do all things": these are little warnings of a shift of tone, little calls for an act of faith in *the Lord* of the here and now. It is the kind of shift one finds in novels of the Victorian era, when loyal servants would whisper that "Master" is behind a project. Closer to home, we have the whisper of John to Peter: "It is the Lord"..."and none of those reclining dared ask him, 'Who art thou?' knowing that it is the Lord" (Jn. 21:7, 12). And there is surely an allusion to Our Lady's vespertime Magnificat when, in common with RM, RB tells us not to let our "good observance" elate us, but rather to "magnify *the Lord* who is operating in us."

St. Benedict, loving Scripture and Tradition as he does, naturally has at his fingertips many a name or title for Christ which will emerge in particular contexts or genres: in speaking of the liturgy, allusion to *our Creator* or *the holy Trinity* is as spontaneous as citation of the *Glory be to the Father* or the *Kyrie eleison*. The metaphor of shepherding is particularly frequent, and if we look beyond the explicit references, we find eight chapters using such terms as "flock," "sheepfold," "sheep," "pastor" and fifteen more using the derivative term, "congregation." Of course, most of this shepherding is done by the abbot and is not a reference to God or Christ, but it reveals a trait common to both human and divine custodians of the monks. The term *householder*, on the other hand, seems to be deliberately confined to God, lest it seem that the abbot's relationship to the monks were that of a landowner to his "familia" of "freeborn children" and "slaves." In this same thrust, even the citation in RM of the fourth commandment becomes in RB an honoring of "all men," avoiding mention of "father" as used of contemporary humans. The abbot is rarely called "father"; he is given rather the foreign synonym, *abbas*; and "paternal reverence" to the seniors uses the foreign term *nonnus*. The Cellarer is to be *"as it were* a father in the monastery," and all things are to be looked for from the (unspecified) "father of the monastery." Spiritual intimacy is more often expressed in terms of the "spiritual senior" or "prior" than of the "spiritual father." Spiritual sonship, scarcely developed on the human level, is barely mentioned in regard to God, outside the passages from the RM in the Prologue. By contrast with this vocabulary of the "familia," the term *house of God* and its derivative *domestics of the Faith* come surprisingly often and in key contexts (cellarer, guests, abbatial election). The motives for avoiding the theme of fatherhood are not clear; certainly there was no desire to reverse the transition from slavery to sonship mentioned in Gal. 4:7; but I would suggest a motivation similar to that of the avoidance of "householder" (*pater familias*) for the abbot and the warning lest the abbot take to his own credit those titles given him out of "honor and love of Christ" (RB 63:13). A remarkable continuation of this evolution occurs in St. Stephen Harding of Citeaux who, even more than RM and RB, literally applies Mt. 23:9 to all living men and will give the title "father" only to his deceased forebears; few themes in his writings so contrast with the radical reversal of his successor, Bl. Raynard, as does this one, for he had grown up in the ranks whereas the latter was elected in from elsewhere and imposed upon the prestigious community of Citeaux. He needed to stress his dignity as father. Possibly some equally human and historical factor lies behind RB's reticence with paternal and filial terminology even in regard to God, but we must not overlook his non-use of such other key titles for Christ as "Redeemer," "Savior," "Teacher," to say nothing of "Son of God."

c) Lordship and Servanthood, Kingship and Soldiery

In the beautiful opening passage of the Prologue, peculiar to RB, Christ is named as "the Lord Christ, the true King," for whom the addressee is about to act as "soldier." The same combination of lordship and kingship comes in RB 61:10, where it is encouraged that a visiting monk be persuaded to settle down locally "because in every place it is to the one Lord that service is rendered and to the one King, soldiery." The term *Lord,* as we have seen, is fairly widely used in RB, but these are the only uses of *King* in regard to Christ, apart from incidental mentions of the *Kingdom* in the Prologue. On the other hand, the human counterparts of lordship and kingship, namely servanthood and soldiery, run more extensively through the Rule and tend to convince one that lordship and kingship are pivotal to the Christology of RB. On the other hand, it would be absurd to look for a conscious correlation with servanthood every time the term *the Lord* is used in RB, especially in citations from other sources.

The term "servant of Christ" has a long and nuanced history. Several NT books use it in the course of their exhortations to slaves: these are to sublimate their servanthood by directing it to the supreme Lord, Christ. Paul calls himself a "slave" of Christ in Gal. 1:10, and equivalent terms are used of him in the opening words of Romans, Philippians and Titus (see also James, 2 Peter, Jude, and Apocalypse). But already in NT times the title "servant of God" (with its synonyms) was becoming honorific, belonging on the lips of others rather than one's own (Acts 16:17; Heb. 3:5). In this honorific sense, II Dial. uses the title to soften the *purum nomen* of Benedict, usually alternating between *servus/famulus/vir* with the possessives *Dei/Domini/ Christi*; he also uses it of subordinate heroes, such as Maurus and the superior at Terracina. In the chapter headings of II Dial., the term *servus Dei*, or its feminine equivalent, *ancilla Dei*, is regularly used; it is, in fact, an early technical term, much used around St. Augustine, for celibate personnel who attached themselves to churches in a manner analogous to the attachment of slaves to secular estates. Such a meaning survives in RM (vg. 15:51; 16:18; etc.). A quite different meaning is witnessed in St. Athanasius' *Life of Anthony*, where the hero unhesitatingly identifies himself to the Devil as "servant of Christ." There is here a close parallel to the *Christianus* (christiana) *sum* of the various Acts of the Martyrs, presuming that Coptic Christians translated the Greek word *Christian* as *Servant of Christ*, in the same way that Israelites saw themselves as *Children of Israel*. At the end of all this history, however, RB simply does not use the term: the noun *servus* comes in RB only in its civic sense or in explicit simile. Certainly RB restores to the individual members of the community the dignified title of "monk," almost entirely absent from RM, and also the dignity of their seniority, and it recognizes elite monks as *god-fearing*, but none does it "canonize" as "servants of God." However, RB has no such inhibition in using the corresponding verb: *servio*.

The Latin verb *servio* translates two distinct verbs of the Greek NT: not only *douleuo* ("I act the slave") but also *latreuo* ("I worship"). In both RM and RB both senses are represented, but RM directs the bulk of such service immediately to God, whereas RB directs it mainly to the brethren, "as if to Christ." On the few occasions that RM speaks of service to humans, it is either in a civic sense (vg. RM 16:21) or else in an institutional sense (vg. to serve tables, RM 23 T); only in what amounts to a footnote concerning the infirm, almost as an afterthought, does RM 70:1 enjoin that the brethren should "visit, console and *serve*" the sick, so as to fulfill the precept of Mt. 25:36—and here, because of the context, the verb *servio* is forced to govern, not the interpersonal dative case but the more objective accusative. By contrast, RB puts the concept of mutual service into prominence in the opening maxims of pertinent chapters or paragraphs (RB 35:1; 36:1; 53:18), stressing even more explicitly that Christ is the horizon of such service. In fact, while abandoning the religious use of RM's term *servus,* RB goes on to "coin" a noun adapted to this interpersonal use of *servio,* namely *servitor;* RB also downplays RM's neuter noun *servitium* in favor of the feminine *servitus,* but it is difficult to prove an interpersonal stress in this latter change. Such independence in the use of the vocabulary of servanthood does, however, reinforce the special meaning we found in RB's use of *the Lord,* particularly in contexts of a hushed reference to Providential intervention. It goes without saying that both Rules also use the vocabulary of serving to designate abusive allegiances to "self-will" and other false lords; by a certain, perhaps unconscious, punning, this divergent allegiance is also named with the verb *servare* ("to maintain, to keep up").

Then there is the military metaphor, which presents Christ as King and us as his soldiers. The noun *soldier,* though used four times in RM, is absent from RB, where only the verb *milito* and its abstract noun *militia* are used. In RM, the basic sense of "soldiery" is close to our modern concept of "ascesis" or of "practicing," as when a physician "practices" medicine. Like *servire, militare* can, in RM, name a soldiering done for the Devil as well as for the "school of the Lord," for "obedience" as well as for one's "own preference." Three such texts of RM survive in RB, but the military metaphor in these passages could just as well be replaced by one of servanthood or workmanship; we must

look rather to the texts where RB uses the military metaphor independently if we would profit by the light it
throws on the Christology of RB. These are the two texts
we have already seen, at the beginning of the Prologue and
in the exhortation to a visiting monk, and there is also the
little formula addressed to the novice after his first hearing
of the Rule: "Behold the Law under which thou wishest to
soldier. . . ." Kingship is explicitly related to the soldiery in
the first two texts; in the third it is perhaps implicit because
of the analogy of the monk's initiation to that of a Roman
soldier, in which the essential element is the oath of allegiance to the Emperor. In itself, RB's use of the term *King* is
too rare to be very instructive, but the co-relationship with
"soldiery" gives us an added source for finding its content,
and the surprising fact that RM never associates kingship
with Christ at all, whereas RB mentions it at such key
points, gives us further assurance of its importance to the
latter.

As for the content of the military metaphor, one would
spontaneously expect a great deal of "fighting," presum-
ably against the Devil and the vices personified, and then a
great deal about weaponry. But, apart from one or two
literal references in RM to secular soldiery, neither Rule
has mention of battle outside of the common chapter on
the Kinds of Monks. There the Latin term is *pugna, pugnare;*
in vain do we search for the synonyms: *bellum, praelium,
certamen,* except in the non-military adverb *certatim,* used of
the striving to outdo one another in punctuality. Of the
few mentions of weaponry, some are simply not part of the
metaphor of soldiery for Christ (*gladium, theca, arcus* in RM;
ferrum in RB); the more generic term *armare* (RM), *arma* (RB)
does refer to spiritual warfare, but for RM it is the Devil or
personified Negligence that arms the human combatant
and uniquely in RB do we find our soldier's true armor:
"Obedience's most sturdy and outstandingly bright
armor," donned precisely by the addressee of the Prologue

who is "about to soldier for the Lord Christ the true King."
This indeed is a key text for all the Christology of RB,
though one might argue for military overtones also in the
Christology, taken from RM, wherein one "dashes infant
thoughts against the Rock which is Christ" and uses the
Sign of the Cross to ward off temptation. But, apart from
that, the vocabulary of defense (*defendo, munio, custodio*) is
one of policing and sentry duty, practiced especially in the
"guard placed over one's mouth"—themes strong in RM
but rarer in RB, and in neither Rule throwing much light
on the royal Christology.

Taking a cue therefore from the key text about the
armor of obedience, I would see the real content of the
military and royal metaphor in terms of the soldier's keen
alertness and readiness for obedient action, and the King's
corresponding mastery of the field. The whole sense of
Gospel "leadership" and of "imitation" and "followership"
—through "suffering" into "glory" and "kingdom"; the
sense of readiness to take injuries in stride; the injunction
that monks should be "ever on the ready," even when in
bed; the declaration that "idleness" is the soul's "enemy";
the horror of negligence, acedia, inertia (*nimis iners...desidi-
osus...acediosus...*); the urge towards complete "abrenun-
ciation" and immediate compliance with orders, along with
the vocabulary of hastening, running, forestalling one
another; the overwhelming occurrence of terms of completeness (all, altogether, always, without intermission,
integrally...): all these trends in RB spell out the meaning
of the military and royal metaphor, implying that the King
being soldiered for is correspondingly alive and alert and
worthy of absolute dedication.

As mentioned above, these metaphors of servanthood
and soldiery should not be read as reversals of the adoption
of sons in Gal. 4:7, even though RB scarcely exploits this
latter theme. Rather, in every metaphor suggested by any
context, RB would have us maximize our investment in

Christ and obtain supreme intimacy: "nothing is to be preferred to the love of Christ." Rather than contrast RB with Gal. 4:7, it is profitable to contrast it with an institution of our own day, the egalitarian commune. I happen to have studied one such commune, Twin Oaks in Virginia. In many ways they put us to shame in their avoidance of detraction, competition, consumerism and in their readiness to love and honor one another. But their egalitarianism prompts horizontal friendships which render servanthood redundant and rule out the use of titles and even the use of elections and the recognition of heroes. There is no analogue of lordship among them, comparable to the derived lordship of the Benedictine abbot, which could offer them a basis to appreciate the lordship of Christ. The contrast with RB does but intensify our awareness of the vertical dimension in the Rule, even down to its physical expression in such gestures as bowing and prostrating. One cannot but think of the search for the last place as a "diving," almost a "ducking under," so as to open up room for the higher place to be occupied by one closer to the Lord, and by the Lord himself. One begins to read RB's "he who humbles himself" in a new parallelism with "he who listens to you": "he who humbles himself ...makes room for the Lord...draws the Lord down into encounter with himself." This humbling of oneself in RB takes on the style of a particular courtesy and a particular deportment, no less revolutionary than those of Twin Oaks, but with far-reaching Christological implications, which we will consider below.

In the meantime, on the intellectual and verbal level, we have found RB sparing in its use of names for Christ, a reverential avoidance which did but heighten those few passages where he whispers a hushed recognition of an intervention of "the Lord," of "*our* Lord," the "Christ dearer" to us than anything, than whose inviting voice nothing could be "sweeter"; yet a kingly Christ, one whose personality is learned most fully when we, in servanthood and soldiery, become the living counterparts of his lordship and royalty.

II: Christ as Looming upon the Horizon

When a military team is aiming a trench mortar, their target is out of sight and they align their viewers upon metal stakes which simulate the direction and the plane of that target. In the same way, to put us into communication with Christ, RB sets up relationships within the monastery which point us in his direction; he himself looms beyond them, upon the horizon. Everyday realities around the monastery thus become landmarks or pointers towards him. Even more explicit is Christ's looming behind the Scriptures, which form the background music of the house. Christ is the horizon of all honor shown by the monks, all love, all courtesy. Finally, Christ is the "deadline" and the goal of that wayfaring haste which seasons the peaceful gravity of the Rule.

a) Everyday Realities Pointing towards Christ

Awareness of the invisible Christ orientates even the tools and utensils of the monastery, prompting not only careful use, regulated guardianship and the making of frequent inventories, but also lining them up with the sacred vessels of the altar. And what a pointer towards Christ the altar itself becomes in RB! Located in the oratory, where nothing alien is done or stored, its table serves to receive the monk's charter of profession as he chants his "Receive me, O Lord," and its drapes serve to wrap the arm of the child being offered by its parents.

There is a similar Christ-ward climaxing in time: the year climaxes at Christ's Easter, with Lent to intensify the build-up; the week climaxes in Sunday, with Wednesdays and Fridays, at least in summer, to serve as quasi-Lents; even in the ferial night office, there is a Christ-ward build-up when the second nocturn switches from antiphons to *Alleluias,* and Lauds soon follows with its climax in the *Benedictus.* The Sunday and festive night office has the Christ-ward crescendo in the readings: OT, NT and Gospel, the last being read by the abbot in person.

Again, in the human hierarchy, while RB is explicitly downplaying the rights of clerics and officers and artisans, it is nevertheless rebuilding the traditional system of seniority so neglected by RM, and the graphic orientation from neophyte to veteran, accentuated at every exchange of courtesy, points unmistakably to Christ. Within the cloister, the abbot acts the role of Christ, but outside the enclosure it is the guest who takes over that role, especially the "domestics of the Faith" and above all the bishop. At a distance looms the "Roman Church" and all the "named and orthodox Catholic Fathers," but always on the horizon there looms Christ himself.

b) Christ Behind the Scriptures

There is one seeming exception to this gradation of all things to Christ in RB, and it is instructive. When RB is assembling Scriptural texts to support an exhortation, one would expect the kind of build-up found in Prol. 30-34: Prophet, Apostle, Lord; but that is the only such case. True, we cannot demand much where we know that RB is abbreviating RM, which is more consistent on this score, but it still surprises us to find a dominical saying sandwiched or followed by afterthoughts from a lesser author (RB 7:32, 42, 65). Often enough RB will acknowledge that it is the Lord who is the speaker, but there are three passages common to both Rules in which the same divine speaker gives an utterance from the Psalms and from the Gospels with no adequate signal to warn of the change (RB Prol. 13; 2:14-5; 5:6). Then again, true dominical sayings are sometimes presented with impersonal expressions like "let him remember *the writ*, mindful of the *divine utter-*

ance..."; others are presented as being from "the (Lord's) Prayer" or the "evangelical (Parable of the) Publican" or are otherwise hinted as being from the Gospels; but quite a number of dominical sayings are used unannounced and even slightly reworded to fit the context. Even in these cases, however, such is the courtesy of St. Benedict towards his Lord that a little shift of tone is often the signal of citation, notably the little "because" in RB 2:30; 27:1. The fact remains, however, that dominical sayings are given less relief than we would expect in RB; indeed, we find even non-canonical sayings introduced as "Scripture" (vg. RB 7:33) or as something that "we read" (RB 18:25; 40:6). There is no doubt that RB orthodoxy ranks the writings of the Fathers below the Scriptures (RB 9:8; 73:2-5), and so great is his reverence for Scripture that satisfaction must be made for any slip in its recitation; moreover, only those are to read it publicly who edify their hearers, and only those parts are to be read which suit the hour of the day (though there is insistence on integral and sequential reading of the Lenten books). The weekly reader, like the artisans and the traveling monks, needs to be purged of the "spirit of elation" by a special Sunday blessing. Perhaps it is this context of objectivity that is the key to the lack of relief for the dominical sayings: the reader, free of elation, disappears and the Scripture itself cries out to us, Scripture personified, the Word in Person, who is Christ. It is one and the same Christ who, in the Psalm, says "Come" and, in the Gospel, says "Run" (Prol. 13): why spoil the literary build-up with a scruple over bibliography? One might as well insist on noting which Gospel, which chapter and verse, which alleged pre-canonical Gospel source.... Just as it is Christ whom we are listening to when we obey the abbot, so it is Christ whom we are responding to when we "willingly snatch up holy readings," regardless of book, chapter or verse. Not only by "diving" vertically to humble himself as a servant does the monk create space for

Christ's presence, but also by "attuning his ears" (RB Prol. 9) he lures the Lord out of his silence into the daily "shouting" of the Scriptures.

c) Christ, the Horizon for Honor, Love and Courtesy

Just as "Lord" and "King" are the key Christological titles in RB, so "honor" and "love" (*amor*) are the key Christological attitudes on our part. Beyond the philological study of these two terms, there are those non-verbal habits evoked by RB, which I gather together under the English term "courtesy."

Honor shown to the visible brother, nay, "to all men," prolongs itself into honor shown to the invisible Christ, but it must be "congruous honor" (RB 53:2). Not only are there the "diabolical illusions" to be avoided by preliminary prayer, but there are the purely human imposters, like Totila's officer in regal attire, for whom St. Benedict does not even rise from his reading (II Dial. 14). Yet, just as the promptings of "human nature" are not despised when the Rule is regulating the care of the aged and the young, so note is duly taken of the "very terror" that the rich inspire and the "humility and reverence" that are spontaneous when we seek an audience and a favor from "mighty men." There is therefore special stress on honoring the poor, yet privileged treatment goes in the end to the "domestics of the Faith." Some of the gestures prescribed in the more theoretical passages on hospitality and mutual deference might strike the modern mind as less than "congruous": the embarrassing washing of the feet, prostration and verse; but the welcome is balanced off with a "showing of all humaneness," a "wise administration by wise men." Individual contact with the guests is minimized, as is the disturbance of the common schedule for their sake, the slack being taken up by the appointed officers. The same applies to the sick; here, in a form much milder than that of RM, RB shows both sides of the coin: it is all very well for the sick to be served as Christ, but it is up to them to feel humbled for the mercy shown them and to be reasonable in their demands. Always, however, there is slack to be taken up, even with a clearly defined system of officership and seniority, and in the taking up of this slack the keynote is to "forestall one another in honor."

It is of the nature of showing honor that one abase oneself and exalt the other; the movement is vertical, placing the recipient on a higher plane. There is a whole series of terms in RB for this upward regard: *reverence, veneration, fear, dread, trembling,*. . .all of which have God as their ultimate object. It is less easy to define the vocabulary of "love" in terms of this vertical thrust, though *amor*, the term used of Christ, is normally upward, a love of admiration and aspiration rather than of pity and of fostering (*pietas,* and some instances of *diligere* and *caritas*). The *amor,* whose horizon is Christ, is also rightly directed to God, to the abbot, to the fraternity as a whole, and to such worthy practices as fasting and progress towards eternal life, but only by abuse does *amor* turn to the vices of much speaking, much laughter, contention and self-will. Ungrounded favoritism by the abbot is also expressed with the otherwise upward term *amor.* This slightly confusing vocabulary of love raises a further question: why does RB have nothing equivalent to a statement that to love one's visible brother is to love the invisible Christ? I would suggest that the answer lies in love's being a disposition rather than an act: one can feed, nurse, welcome Christ in particular human acts, but love penetrates all of these acts and goes beyond them. In fact, in RB, love is as much an end in itself as is the eschatological reward: serving in the kitchen is a deed whence "greater reward *and charity* is acquired" (RB 35:2). In the same way, this charity, an end in itself, is to be "conserved, confirmed, safeguarded and never abandoned" and all the monk's strivings for humility are aimed at his "arrival at perfect charity, which casts out fear." Growth in charity is all-important, and its measure is mentioned in several contexts: "most fervent charity, all dutifulness of charity, equal charity towards all. . . ." While nothing is to be preferred to the *amor* of Christ, and while other tasks are done and other arrangements made for the sake of charity's preservation, still Christ is only to be called the "horizon for charity" in a sense somewhat different from that in which he is the horizon for honor, since charity is itself something of a goal, something of an horizon.

The everyday gestures of honor and charity can be grouped under the English word *courtesy*. We have already seen how the cultivation of humility in RB is directed to making room for the Lord Christ, and how the physical postures mentioned for moments of special humility involve a vertical bowing of the head, the knees, the whole body, almost as if to dive for the lowest place. In the case of prayer away from the oratory, this "diving" is done "with a divine trembling, bending the knees." But it is not purely external, nor purely non-verbal. The effort to forestall one another in honor demands an alert mind and an absence of interior murmuring, of occasions for presumption, of envy, jealousy, pride. . . . There can exist rival atmospheres which counter the upbuilding (*aedificatio*) so desired by the Rule: these include scurrilous yarning, small talk, casual chatter. . .but also sadness. Gravity, indeed, and discipline, but with no one upset or saddened in the house of God! It is a setting in which the individual has his place and keeps to it, but remains ever mindful that he is there only because he has been graciously received in response to his own petition to be associated with the body of the monastery. At every turn his courtesy has him "asking the prayers," "asking a blessing" from those more securely integrated than he. He understands how great a punishment it is to be excommunicated and deprived of the fellowship and participation of oratory and table, to eat alone and to eat food unblessed. He realizes that, should he fall into contrariness (*contrarius existens...et contemptor...*), his only cure would lie in submitting to a measure of humiliation under the arbitration of the local officialdom: he is entirely at their mercy. How aptly the traditional rituals bade the new postulant ask for the "mercy of God and of the Order"! Perhaps even more faithful to RB would be the wording: "your mercy and that of your Lord." Yet, what *worthiness* has this local officialdom that one should submit to it? Just the fact that *Christ* looms upon its horizon: "he who listens to you is listening to me."

d) Christ in the Perspective of the Wayfarer's Haste

One of the relationships RB recognizes between the individual and Christ is that of "imitation," expressed with the Gospel metaphor of "following" him—following him precisely "to glory." This metaphor takes on graphic detail in the course of the Rule, where the goal is described in the upward terms: *peak, loftiness, topmost, heavenly fatherland...*; and the road is described in the grueling terms: *narrow way, straight course, rough and rugged...*; and the gait is described as one of *hastening, running, progressing....* This grueling way-faring brings into play all the alertness that we found in the concept of soldiering for Christ, but the purpose of it all is to enable us to see him in his kingdom, "him who has called us." The urgency of the wayfaring stems from the uncer-tainty of the outcome, which hinges entirely upon Christ's judgment of us: in every temptation we face a fork in the road, one branch leading to life and the other to Gehenna. There is also a concept of "backsliding," which is done "through the sloth of disobedience," but otherwise failure is seen as a deviation from the "narrow way." The Christ of this wayfaring is not only its goal; he himself first trod it for us. It is through patient participation in his sufferings that we become consorts of his glory.

And yet the following of Christ to glory is nothing other than "persevering in his doctrine in the monastery until death," "never departing from his mastership." In this monastery he looms daily as the horizon of the most ordinary realities, be it the tools or the quotations from Scripture or the chance encounters with brethren in need. Small wonder that one who so hovers around the house should sometimes be discerned intervening in its affairs—and "no one dare ask 'Who art thou?' knowing it is the Lord."

III: Christ as "Spectator" and as God of Surprises

We read in II Dial. 3:5 that, when St. Benedict left the monks who had tried to poison him, he returned to his cave and "solus in superni *spectatoris* oculis habitavit secum"— "alone and at home with himself in the eyes of his lone Spectator on high." Awareness of spectators, visible and invisible, is part of the Christology of RB, but the invisible one is not so aloof that he cannot be addressed and asked to intervene; indeed, his interventions can be full of surprises.

a) "Spectators" in RB, Visible and Invisible

The concept of God's observing us is frequent in RM, and RB takes over a number of pertinent such passages. RM has further invisible spectators in the person of the angels, but RB is more sparing in mention of these; they do occur, however, in one biblical text in a florilegium on dispositions for psalmody. But far more central to RB are those visible human spectators who share something of the dignity of that "lone spectator on high." RM too has its sensitivity to human spectators, but in quite different directions: on the one hand there are dramatic tableaux, especially at meals, but on the other there is a self-conscious hiding of the "secret of the monastery" from such seculars as it would prompt to either flattery or mockery of the brethren, but more central to the thought of RM is the human spectatorship or supervision done by the deans. These supervisors are spectators to the individual's every move, ready to pounce on him with a Scriptural quotation for the tiniest slip. Even allowing for the literary genre, such close supervision would seem to stifle the Holy Spirit. It is doubly interesting to see how RB handled the heritage of the deaneries while also restoring the system of seniority, for his handling of that obsolescent institution involved adjustments of his own Christology which may have lessons for us as we cope with the short-lived experimental structures of our post-conciliar era.

RB certainly did much to liberate the individual from excessive human supervision, but in some ways the rejection of self-will is even more radical in RB than in RM: individuals can indeed be recognized as wise, God-fearing, mature, etc., but "neither their bodies nor their wills are at their own disposal," and they must "look to the father of the monastery for everything," "feeling humbled for the mercy thus shown to them" and "asking a blessing" at every turn. This is the radical dependence upon the community at large and upon its officialdom in particular, of which we spoke above. At Subiaco St. Benedict had had deans, who may well have been as stifling as those of RM, but when he wrote RB he showed a twofold evolution: firstly, rather than wait to be pounced upon by the human spectator, the monk was expected spontaneously to confess his faults and, secondly, RB was concerned to expose the delinquent to the eyes of the community at large. Confession is now made to a "spiritual senior," who is either the abbot, acting the role of Christ, or else a senior, perhaps chosen for the individual with his own personal needs in mind. As for the exposure to the community at large, it fits in with St. Benedict's esteem for the wishes of the community at large in such matters as appointment of officers: Christ somehow operates through that choice— and also through the merciful eyes which thus take account of the delinquent's repentance and satisfaction. The Christology here is the same as we saw for excommunication in the paragraph on courtesy above. In these contexts, RB regularly uses the words *public, publicly, in front of all,* but, strange as it may seem, such expressions are entirely absent from RM, except for such secular settings as towns and inns and for the ceremony of abbatial blessing, where the witnessing community is immediately diluted by mention of the "whole of mankind" and even of "God." For RM, the assembled community is scarcely sacramental for the individual, whereas such sacramentality is vital to the Christology of RB. The contrast in the use of *publicly* holds also for *secretly*; RM has, as we saw, "family affairs" that are kept secret from outsiders, but only in RB do we find a developed concern for secrecy in the healing of hidden sins, and in the preliminary warnings to those risking excommunication, and in the kindly offices of the *synpectae* who befriend those actually excommunicated, and in the individual's additional prayers in the oratory. All this secrecy in RB amounts to a recognition of the value we moderns call "privacy," though the actual term *private* has a slightly pejorative ring in RB, where its use ranges from "de-privation" of table fellowship to unofficial orders competing with official ones and on to ferial days as contrasted with Sundays. But the interplay of the "secret" and the "public," based as it is on Mt. 18:15-16 (RB 23:2) represents a series of juridical instances that point towards the judgment seat of Christ. Hence it is that one approaches that "public" as closely as possible to profess one's vows, to confess one's sins and to hear oneself berated for one's unrepentance.

c) Christ as the God of Surprises

This article has dealt with the human counterparts of Christ's presence and has had little to say of Christ in himself. It would be too vast and too distinct a topic to develop the latter; suffice it therefore to mention that one would need to juxtapose Christ with the Father and the Holy Spirit—not an easy task in RB—and with the angels and the devil, the flesh and the secular world. There would be the devil's "persuading" action to consider and also Christ's "help" and God's "protection." We would need to see just what it means to "fling our infant thoughts against the rock which is Christ," and what it is to engage in "most instant prayer" to him, to offer ourselves or our children for his acceptance, and especially to commend to him the absent brethren and the incorrigible delinquent. Of even greater interest would be those providential interventions which we saw, and about which RB whispered to us, as John did to Peter, that "it is the Lord." In the meantime, one thing is clear: nothing is to be preferred to the love of Christ, a Christ we do not see here below as he is in himself, but the Rule was written in order to help us come to "see him in his Kingdom."

A PERSONAL CHRISTOLOGY

William Meninger, OCSO

*(Monk of St. Benedict's Monastery,
Snowmass, Colorado)*

For many years I have had a somewhat fanciful vision of
heaven immediately after death. I think, however, that it
contains a large element of truth. I shall close my eyes,
after whatever lethal preliminaries are my destiny, and in
an instant open them again. In the face of all previous fear,
wonder and speculation, I will look upon the visage of an
old, familiar friend and gasp, "Why, I know you!" Hope-
fully what I shall see will be the face of Jesus, a face that I
have seen thousands of times in this life; a person that I
have served, prayed with and for, counseled, visited,
clothed, fed, and buried. But even more significantly, I
shall see a person who has counseled me, served me,
clothed and fed me in the myriad faces of all his ministers,
recognized hitherto only in faith, but now in knowledge
and understanding.

I shall know then even as I am known. However, it still
remains true that even now, I do know and I do understand
in part, albeit obscurely. My Christology, my understanding and experience of who the Christ is, which will be
completed only in the event of my definitive salvation, is in
process now. It began whenever it was that Jesus first
addressed those challenging words to me, "Who do *you* say
that I am?" and goes on as long as I continue to reach out
and grasp the victory that he has won for me.

The Book of Revelation tells me that the Lord has a
hidden name reserved for me that only he knows. Only he
knows my real self, the true me, the me that I shall become
under the guidance of his grace and the final gift of his
salvation. But he himself has a hidden name that it is my

goal in life (and death) to discover. This is my personal
Christology—the real theology—to experience, meditate
upon and come to an understanding and response to who
this Jesus Christ is. This is my process toward the real me!

In his *Interim Report on the Books Jesus and Christ* (Crossroad,
NY, 1981), Edward Schillebeeckx says that Christian
theology depends upon two sources which have a mutually
critical correlation. The first is the tradition of the Jewish-
Christian movement (the Old and New Testaments), and
the second is the contemporary, new, human experiences
of Christians and non-Christians, i.e., the situation we
live in today, and which is an intrinsic and determinative
element in comprehending God's revelation. (To avoid
copious footnotes, much of the following theory on Christology is taken from Schillebeeckx's book. The application
of it to a personal Christology is my own.)

God has revealed in the Scriptures, but our understanding of this revelation depends heavily on the Church's
experience of it and, like Mary, her subsequent pondering
over it in her heart. It follows then that understanding
revelation (another name for which is theologizing) will be
an ongoing process following from ever new experiences,
needs, and situations confronted by the Church during her
earthly pilgrimage. While it remains true that the Church
is something more than the mere sum of her parts, it is
equally true, as Nicholas of Cusa maintains, that each one
of us is the Church (somehow in its entirety) and any
personal Christology partakes of and contributes to the
Church's Christology.

During the '60s it was a popular gimmick for newspapers
to hold religious surveys in which Catholics (and others)
would be asked such fundamental questions as: "Do you
believe in the soul, the Trinity, the divinity of Christ, etc."
The answers were usually disconcerting to anyone with a
smattering of theology (why else would the newspapers
ask them?), and if any understanding of an authentic

Christology were to be gleaned from them, the Church is in trouble indeed. We must keep in mind here two things; one, to have a Christology one must have a personal experience of the Christ, only then can he or she authentically speculate on it or seek to interpret it; and two, this experience and interpretation must have a critical correlation to the tradition of the Jewish-Christian movement, i.e., it must stand up to and be measured by Scriptural revelation as preserved in the community of the Church (including the Councils).

There are many Christologies, even and especially in the context of revelation itself. We no longer see the Gospels as biographies of Jesus but rather as interpretations. Just a look at the first two or three verses of each Gospel will demonstrate how they each start off with a Christology. John interprets Jesus as the pre-existing Logos; Mark, as the fulfillment of the Messianic prophecies of the Old Testament. Even a swift perusal of the names or titles given to Jesus in the Gospels will also reveal further interpretations: Son of David, Son of Man, Lord, Lamb of God, etc. Other Christologies are seen in the writings of St. Paul, in Hebrews, and in Revelation. Some of these are Spirit-inspired revelations coming from an individual (personal Christologies), others from a community. One has only to observe how St. Paul's conversion influenced his interpretation of Christ or how Mark's understanding of his community's needs in time of persecution affected his Gospel.

The Christologies of the New Testament as read and prayed and pondered over by the Church are normative. One manifestation of the Church's ongoing Christology is the Councils. Even though, e.g., Chalcedon's Christology took on a definitive form, the process itself is still ongoing, and further Christologies, personal or not, have to be seen in relation to the influence of the Spirit on a given age as well as to the decisions of past Councils (at least they may not contradict them). This may result sometimes in an effort to compare cabbages with kings. Nonetheless it must be done. Schillebeeckx warns though that there is a danger of focusing on certain interpretative elements from the past rather than on the issue of salvation itself.

The last word about Jesus has not been said. Indeed it cannot be said until the last man or woman is asked to respond to the question, "Who do you say that I am?" As Schillebeeckx maintains, contemporary experience, both of the Church and of individuals in it, is a determinative element for understanding Christ. It is the purpose of the Church's teaching to develop effectively the particular meanings that being a Christian today implies. The Christian tradition in its beginnings was not a doctrine but an experience, a question of interpretative perception. The scribes experienced Jesus differently from the apostles, again a question of interpretative perception.

We also as individuals have to reflect upon our own experiences. When the history of the Christian experience is appropriated to ourselves then we have a living tradition. The interpretations we place on our experience of Christ look then to the Scriptures and to the Church's response to the Scriptures. But we must fully admit and accept the fact that there are also interpretative elements which come from other sources, e.g., the social sciences and even the reflections and reactions of non-Christians on Christ. In the course of 2000 years of living tradition, interpretative elements have accumulated continuously as Christians have attempted to express their experience of grace in Christ.

Let us glance briefly at a few interpretations of Jesus popular recently to see different interpretative elements at work (for more material on this matter cf. John Shea, *The Challenge of Jesus*, p. 25, par. 2. Image, paperback, 1977). The Jesus of *Superstar* is radically different from the clown of *Godspell*. The Lord of Kazentzakis' *The Last Temptation of*

Christ, is hardly the harlequin of Harvey Cox. In the Church's past history, we also see the troubadour simplicity of the Christ of St. Francis, the stark poverty of Charles de Foucauld's Jesus, the loving bridegroom of St. Bernard, the majestic king of St. Teresa of Avila, and the kindly father of St. Therese.

As Father John Shea writes (*ibid.,* pg. 25):

> ...to attempt an exhaustive appraisal of Jesus in a single image subtly undermines the richness of divine activity connected with his life. Jesus lived out of a transcendence which first reduces humankind to wondering silence and then to a riot of metaphors. Images explore this mystery of Jesus but in no way exhaust it. Further, Jesus-imaging is the way Western people ask the meaning of life. The many Jesuses are personal and collective searches for a cause to be committed to, a passion to be consumed by, a life which has worth and purpose. Explorations into Jesus are not only historical expeditions but the way the self asks its deepest questions.

There is, of course, the danger of using Jesus as a propaganda tool. Thus we see, for example, the Marxist Jesus carrying a rifle. This sort of thing happens when the current ideology is adopted instead of being confronted. Current myths and assumptions should not control what is said, rather the controlling perspective has to be a Jesus critiqued by the New Testament and the Church's tradition. Only in this way can we avoid recreating Jesus in our own image and likeness.

How do we go about forming our own personal Christology? Keeping in mind what has been said regarding the normative role of the Church's teaching, there are a number of helpful questions we can ask which might aid us in forming our present Christology. Perhaps the first thing might be to write down in a few paragraphs our "off the cuff" answer to the question of Jesus, "Who do you say that I am?" Then after answering some further questions and after some further pondering in prayer on the subject, we could listen to the question asked again and rewrite our answer.

The following questions might be helpful also. List ten adjectives that you feel best describe the characteristics of Jesus as you have experienced him. Note especially the ones that come most readily to mind, i.e., the first three or four. Are they demanding or giving qualities? Do they serve to encourage the development of your capacities as a fully human person? Which of the many titles given Jesus in the New Testament is your favorite? Why? Which do you find least attractive? Why? What person, parable, incident in the New Testament do you most readily identify with? Why? What was Jesus' reaction to the same person or incident? Write down two or three of the most significant conversion or grace-filled experiences you have had and relate them to Jesus as you presently understand him. Does your understanding of Jesus differ today from your understanding of him five or ten years ago? How? How would you have answered the question, "Who do you say that I am?" ten years ago?, twenty years ago? What is your understanding of the Church as the Body of Christ? To what extent does the rest of the world share in this concept? How does this influence your practical daily activity? your reaction to the daily news? your prayer life? What does it mean to you to say that Jesus is your personal Savior? that he has won the victory for you? How does Jesus, as you understand him from the New Testament, mediate the Father for you? Is your understanding of God different from what it might have been without Jesus? How? Do you see Jesus as judge primarily or as an understanding friend? (Do not answer the way you would *want* to but the way you actually see him.) Describe Jesus in one page to a Jew who knows nothing of him, to a pagan, to a nominal Christian, to a devout Christian, to a child, to your father or mother. Does the fact of the Jesus-event make any difference to you when confronting the problem of evil? especially of innocent suffering in the abstract? in your own personal suffering? What is the difference between Jesus and the Christ? (remember, these are not questions of theory but of your own experience or feelings). What saints or prophets living or dead, best embody the reality of Jesus in their own lives in your opinion? How? What three individuals that you know personally best embody for you the Spirit of Jesus? How? Is the Christ we worship today different from the Jesus you know from Scriptures? Is the Jesus of liturgical worship different from the Jesus of your private prayer? How? Formulate verbally or in writing a prayer to the Father in which you express your doubts and/or questions about the role of Jesus in your life. Conclude it with an expression of gratitude for the specific influences Jesus has had for you. Let this prayer be as long as need be—even extending over several days. It might be interesting to compare your answers with those of a close friend.

There are indeed many images of Jesus, many Christologies. Each one of us who has experienced in faith his saving grace and has reflected upon this salvation also has a Christology. It would even seem that the pondering is a necessary response to that grace. The more explicit we can make our own understanding or perception of our grace-experience, the more efficacious it can be. Even this, however, is an ongoing experience, as the question: "Who do you say that I am?" is asked of us many times. Only by constantly answering it on a personal level will we be able to say one day—when the veil of faith is finally removed— "Why, I know you!"

WHAT CHRIST MEANS TO ME

Felicitas Corrigan, OSB

*(Stanbrook Abbey,
Worcester, England)*

Dear Mother Mary Clare,

During your recent visit to Stanbrook, you engaged me just outside your cell in a conversation that went something like this:

"Would you contribute an article to *Word & Spirit* on your own personal Christology?"

"Please, Mother, would you define 'Christology' in words of one syllable?"

"Yes. Will you write an article on what Christ means to you?"

"Good gracious, how can I possibly say what Christ means to me? He's the very air I breathe, and you don't stop to define or analyze breath, do you, apart from the fact that it is necessary to life?"

"Exactly. Say so, will you? Ten to twelve typewritten pages. You needn't feel bound to a deadline, so long as I can have it before January. Thank you!"

The dulcet voice would obviously not take No for an answer. Nothing for it but to trust in God's help and go straight ahead. Yet I feel wholly inadequate. Incapable of abstract thought, I have no knowledge whatever of philosophy or metaphysics, and today's theological dialectic leaves me, as Sam Weller said, "what the Italians call reg'larly flummoxed." Not for me to discourse of "existential proclivities," to explore a "Jesus decisive for self-understanding," or to "vindicate political and social reform as a proper implication of the Christian understanding of freedom" (I quote from the *Times Literary Supplement* of September 24, 1982). To me, none of this spells Christ, Lord and Savior. Well, what does? you may ask.

A lapidary phrase of St. Augustine sums up my attitude: "This is my life: to praise Thee." It goes hand in hand with my favorite psalm-verse: *Quid enim mihi est in coelo, et a te quid volui super terram? Defecit caro mea et cor meum, Deus cordis mei, et pars mea Deus in aeternum.* (Whom have I in heaven but thee? And there is nothing upon earth that I desire besides thee. My flesh and my heart may fail, but God is the strength of my heart and my portion for ever. [Ps. 72:25-26].) He is the Christ and God of the Bible, not of the textbook of dogmatic theology. If the best part of Shakespeare's best plays is the vast and serene personality of Shakespeare himself, then infinitely truer is it that the best part of the Scriptures, from the first page of Genesis to the last of the Apocalypse, is the Word of God in Person. When he came to earth clothed in flesh, he spoke words outwardly plain even to the dullest, but they are words which conceal enigmas and mysteries, to be interpreted throughout a lifetime by those to whom the Holy Spirit gives the key to spiritual realities. For God's word is no mere vibration of air forming consonants and vowels: it calls for an answering resonance in the heart of the listener. Our Lord uses the common things of everyday life: he speaks of bride and bridegroom, father, mother, son, daughter, rich, poor, bread, wine, fire, cloud, thunder, lightning, stone, fish, mountains, birds, flowers, the four points of the compass —and all the time, he is talking in parable and riddle, as if deliberately to veil his own divine glory as God and Creator. *Lectio divina,* as we call it in monastic usage, demands courage, for we walk deliberately into the Divine Unknown, aware that many hard things may be required of us to whom so much is given. But only a foolish reader would imagine he comprehended fully the seemingly clearest statement.

This is where the liturgy comes to one's aid, for the

breviary, missal, sacraments, are inexhaustible store-
houses of teaching and interpretation. The opposition
of psalms, Scriptural readings, commentaries, prayers,
possibly unrelated at first sight, coalesce to form a unity,
filled with a common meaning and significance, all con-
verging on the Christ of revelation. So I am content to
admire from a distance the parterre gardens laid out by
theologians in neat rectangular flower-beds of analysis
and synthesis, and prefer to blaze my own trail through
the thickets of the liturgical ground with its profusion of
symbol, parable and metaphor, all powerfully communicating divine truth without subjecting me to fact-grinding or
logical method. No human insight, of course, can be other
than partial so, quelling my feelings of despair, I shall try to
put something down, even though words of their very
nature obscure and blunt the edge of the very truth one is
trying to express.

In retrospect, the central ideas moulding my approach to
Christ our Lord have been with me since childhood. From
infancy, "our blessed Lord" was cognate with God, the God
who made me, and "made me to know, love and serve him
in this world, and be happy with him for ever in the next."
The words came tripping off my tongue, for Penny Catechism drill went with the baby's bath and its unchanging
lullaby, "I'll sing a hymn to Mary, the Mother of my God."
Truth was absolute and as plain as a pikestaff. At three or
four years of age, my greatest treasure was a holy picture
of our Lord, framed in crystal glass. Night prayers said, I
stood before it "to learn him off by heart." This was
immensely important: I must recognize him the moment I
saw him. He had a thin face with red-gold hair that led to a
beard terminating in two curious curls, and he was dressed
"a little bit funny" in a pale-green tunic and pink cloak
spangled with golden stars. Of course he was God, and
that's how they dressed in heaven. I closed my eyes tight to
stamp him indelibly on my mind. Yes, when I died, I'd

recognize him all right. So I climbed into bed, knelt facing the pillows, draped the top sheet over my head, clasped it firmly under my chin to make a veil, plopped down, played nuns, held my breath—why wait to die?—gasped, and fell asleep murmuring happily, "for ever...and ever...and ever." It was a sad day when reason asserted its claims. So strong was my reaction that when my picture lost all charm, I became apophatic for the rest of my life. When I stopped playing at nuns and became one, I found myself completely at home with *The Cloud of Unknowing*, "for a naked intent directed unto God, without any other cause than himself, sufficeth wholly." I have referred always to "our Lord," yet that does not seem the current usage either in England or America. Here I face a problem which I propose to set out: What name to give to him whom the author of *The Cloud* calls "our lovely Lord Jesus Christ, King of kings and Lord of lords who, among all the sheep of his pasture graciously would choose me to be one of his specials, and set me in this place of pasture"?

In his *Hymn to God*, St. Gregory of Nazianzen asks:

Bearer of all names, how shall I name you—
You alone, the Unnameable?
You who are beyond, beyond all!—
No other name befits you.

God's own arresting revelation to Moses on Mount Horeb, I AM WHO AM, later particularized in Isaiah's "...his name will be called Wonderful Counsellor, Mighty God, Everlasting Father, Prince of Peace" was finally etched in sharp relief by St. Matthew's "...you shall call his name Jesus." It is significant that whereas the evangelists speak simply of "Jesus," the historical figure who they learned by slow degrees was the Messiah and recognized to be God only after his resurrection, St. Paul, who knew none but the risen Lord, uses very different terms. He can scarcely mention Christ Jesus, or Christ crucified, or our Lord Jesus

Christ, without breaking into ecstatic praise of him who is the Power and Wisdom of God. Why, then, during the last two or three decades, have so many reverted to the use of the plain name "Jesus" in exegesis, theology and sermon? Half a century ago such a manner of speech, at least in England, would have stamped the speaker as a Low Church disciple of John Wesley. I am not sufficiently familiar with American practice: Wesley personally appointed his superintendents to New York, and left over 43,000 Methodists in the USA at his death, but I don't know how powerful their influence over the language was. Does it greatly matter how we refer to Christ our Lord? I think it does. *Lex orandi lex credendi.* May there not be an element of real danger in the exclusive use of the simple historical name? May I argue it out for a few minutes, simply because it disturbs me so?

There would seem to be valid reasons for a departure from tradition just at present. The Second Vatican Council reaffirmed a fact largely ignored for centuries, namely, that truth must be felt and experienced before it can be really apprehended. So the post-Conciliar stress is on a God incarnate, a God capable of being known and loved, a God who twice in the Gospels declared the rapture of his union with humanity: *Hic est Filius meus dilectus in quo mihi bene complacui.* In the mysterious words of our Lord, quoted by Matthew and Luke, "Where the body is, there the eagles are gathered together" (Mt. 24:28; Lk. 17:37). God is not merely a spirit endowed with certain attributes. Christianity is concerned with a Being of flesh and blood, a God-Man who took his body from a human mother. Many Christians of today therefore would rather think of the risen body than of the immortal soul, of Christ our Brother, kith and kin, rather than *Rex et Judex Justus:*

> In a flash, at a trumpet crash,
> I am all at once what Christ is, since he was what I am, and

This Jack, joke, poor potsherd, patch, matchwood, immortal diamond,
   is immortal diamond.

Yes, there are valid reasons for the use of the holy Name pure and simple. I am not of course treating here of private prayer, for to any true Christian the name Jesus is a magnet. The Incarnation is not a mere historical event, it is renewed in the body of every one who receives the Holy Eucharist: "My heart and my flesh have rejoiced in the living God."

Having admitted all that, I challenge the use of the plain name as being alien to immemorial Catholic custom. From the outset, England's spiritual formation has been patristic and Benedictine. It is worth recalling that even the term "our Lord" applied solely to Jesus Christ dates no further back than the Book of Common Prayer and the Authorized Version of the Bible. By thus narrowing its association, the reformers forfeited a deep theological insight. Fisher, More, and the Rheims translators follow Walter Hilton and the medieval writers in rendering the Vulgate *Dominus* or even *Deus* (without any possessive pronoun) as "our Lord" or more often "our Blessed Lord," even in translation from the Old Testament. *Spiritus ante faciem nostram christus dominus* (Lam. 4:20) which literally refers to Zedechiah who, as anointed King, was "the breath of our nostrils" is translated by Hilton: "Our Lord Christ is a spirit before our face." Even in such a highly personal outpouring as Richard Rolle's *Song of Love-longing to Jesus* he never departs from this tradition:

Jhesu, God sonn, Lord of majeste...
Jhesu, my God, Jhesu my keyng...
Swete Lord Jhesu Cryst...

The treatment of our Lord's suffering in the eighth century *Dream of the Rood* is typically English:

> Then I saw Man's Lord
> Hasten with great courage, intent on climbing me...
> Then the young warrior—it was God Almighty—
> Stalwart, resolute, stripped himself; climbed the high gallows.

The Ruler, the Lord of heaven, the Son of God, Christus Miles, Imperator—it is the tone and temper of the greatest Processional hymn of all time, the sixth century *Vexilla Regis*. This tradition, with its determined contemplation of the Divine Person in whom the fullness of Godhead dwells bodily, has persisted from Bede and Cynewulf to the mid-twentieth century. Their whole attitude is crystallized most strikingly in Julian of Norwich's vision of "our courteous Lord God" in his Passion. She sees the red blood running down beneath the garland of thorns, but hastens to add: "And in the same shewing, suddenly the Trinity fulfilled my heart most of joy.... For the Trinity is God. God is the Trinity, the Trinity is our Maker, the Trinity is our Keeper, the Trinity is our endless joy and bliss, by our Lord Jesus Christ and in our Lord Jesus Christ. For when Jesus appeareth, the Blessed Trinity is understood as unto my sight."

Once, as a novice, I noticed the deep distress of my novice-mistress, a contemplative of the first rank. Brash young thing that I was, I knocked and entered her cell without more ado. She was sitting in tears, an open breviary on her lap, and at sight of the unwelcome intruder said coldly that she was saying her Office and did not wish to be disturbed. Nothing abashed, with my eyes on the breviary, I countered: "You are not saying your Office. You are saying the 21st psalm. Please, Mother, tell me, what's the matter?" At this, all annoyance vanished, her voice changed, and she replied: "To think that all during the Passion, there was not a ripple over the surface of the Blessed Trinity." Could anything be more directly in the line of the fourteenth century Julian? Mention of Dame Joanna Hopkins has brought me to my own entry into the monastic life and the land of vision, but before I pass on, I should like to ask three awkward questions:

1. Does the fashion of 'Jesus' *tout court* derive from the propositions of Dr. Albert Schweitzer, whose *Quest of the Historical Jesus* (1910) and studies of Pauline theology (1912 and 1931) have had such a powerful impact upon German, American and English Protestant thought? As so often in the past, are Catholics tagging behind, reaping the harvest of the dubious theses advanced by the glamorous organist-physician of Lambaréné?

2. May the plain Name be yet one more manifestation of the craze for democratization? The media, with their massive influence to shape thought and language, use 'Jesus' exactly as they use Plato, Buddha, Mahatma Gandhi, or the latest pop-star, for purposes of entertainment. The simple name is completely neutral—it expresses neither belief nor disbelief, for to speak otherwise would be a vulgar admission of dissociation from a post-Christian scientific world.

3. May the constant use of the unadorned Holy Name among Catholics today witness to the conciliatory attitude towards a prevalent over-emphasis of the horizontal dimension which, in religion, may tend to neglect, then forget, and finally deny the invisible and eternal dimension?

I hope the digression has not been too tedious: I pass on with relief to the liturgical year through which our Lord reveals himself in his mysteries. To me, it takes the form of a triangle of three pivotal points: at the summit, Easter supported by two feasts at the base, that of the Mother of God on January 1, when our nine foundresses made their Solemn Profession at Cambrai in 1625; and the annual commemoration of the Dedication of our monastic church under the title of Our Lady of Consolation on September 6, 1871. All three are closely interwoven, but each has its own special magic. So much has been written about the centrality of the Paschal triduum that one hesitates to add anything further. But in our house Maundy Thursday, a day of pure agape, sees the thirteenth chapter of St. John in action—Christ in our midst, and we celebrating the birth-day of the chalice and of all priests throughout the world, whose hands are empowered to consecrate it anew: *Potestas enim erat in manibus Christi.* (Carmelites are not the only nuns who pray for priests!) The abbess, holding the place of Christ as the Rule ordains, washes the feet of twelve of her nuns, and then moves down the ranks in the refectory to serve each with a portion of food garlanded with tiny nosegays of violets, wild anemones, blue borage, prim-roses, golden celandines, all the wealth of Spring glory. The climax however is reached, naturally enough, in the evening Sacrifice of the Mass. Never do I feel the power of consecrated virginity at the heart of the Church as on Holy Thursday, that power already evident at the Last Supper in the virginal John, leaning on Jesus' bosom. In his *Expositio in Lucam* lib. II 87-88, St. Ambrose writes: *Veniat ergo Deus, aedificet mulierem, illam quidem adjutricem Adae, hanc vero Christi . . . . Veni, Domine Deus, aedifica mulierem istam, aedifica civitatem. Ecce mulier omnium mater, ecce domus spiritalis . . . haec diligitur a Christo quasi sponsa gloriosa, sancta, immaculata . . . . Haec enim est spes Ecclesiae*—"Let God then come, let him build woman, one woman Adam's helpmate, but this one Christ's. Come, Lord God, build such a woman, build the city of God. See her now, this woman who is mother of all; see her, the abode of the Spirit; see her, Christ's beloved, a glorious bride, holy and spotless. This woman is the hope of the Church." One of the tragedies of our day has been the almost incredible defection of so many nuns, unparalleled surely in the history of the Church.

At this point and although not directly connected with the subject under discussion, I am tempted to digress for a few moments, turn to the question of clerical celibacy, and ask: Why is the priesthood so often conceived of today in terms of office rather than of consecration? A young nun with whom I had discussed the topic recently put into my hand this note: "I have just read in Anscar Vonier's *A Key to the Doctrine of the Eucharist* this argument against over-spiritualizing the Incarnation. 'The sacrifice of the Cross,' he writes, 'is not primarily definable in terms of spirit but in terms of the body; it is not the heroic fortitude of Christ on the Cross which constitutes the sacrifice, but the material fact—we need not hesitate to use the word—of the pouring out of the Blood. There is in the sacrifice of the Cross, as well as in the ancient sacrifices, an element of absolute stability, the body of the victim. . . . Everything that constitutes the sanctity and the holiness of the victim is a direct addition to the value of the sacrifice.' He then summarizes Thomas Aquinas—that the holiness of the victim consists in (i) a flesh without blemish, without sin; (ii) the charity of the one offering his flesh. The celebrant at Mass is so intimately linked with the offering of Christ that he stands *in persona Christi,* doesn't he? And that seems to entail a fundamental share in the same offering, 'This is my Body, which is given for you.' I am not convinced by arguments for priestly celibacy based on freedom from worldly cares (1 Cor. 7:32-34), or on a simple reflection in the material realm of spiritual *puritas cordis,* but Vonier's words suddenly presented a *priestly* reason that seems very much more telling."

The Blessed Eucharist, the priesthood, our Lady, the human soul—they are all facets of the same mystery, but before leaving the Mass there is one small point I'd like to make. Hebrews has always been my favorite Epistle. I love the opening fanfare of trumpets: "God who, at sundry times and in divers manners, spoke in times past to the fathers by the prophets, in these days has spoken to us by his Son. . . called by God a high priest according to the order of Melchisedech." Melchisedech, that mysterious priest of El-Elyon, King of justice, King of peace (Heb. 7:2) is a fascinating figure. With his symbolic prophetic offering of bread and wine he stands alongside Abel holding in his arms the sacrificial lamb in the Canon of the Mass, to show forth that the Lamb, the "I am before Abraham was" has been "slain from the beginning." Since the Council, we have become much more aware of the spiritual experiences of millions who have never known or accepted the Judaeo-Christian revelation, and in the two figures of Abel and Melchisedech, the Christian priesthood with their "merciful and faithful high priest," build a bridge that unites cosmic religion and Catholic worship so that, from the eternal standpoint, temples, sacred groves, pagan priests and worshippers, are all drawn into the orbit of the Mass and find in it their fulfillment.

It is but a short step from the Bethlehem, the "House of Bread" of the Mass to the Mother of the Lamb of God, the Word made flesh, and I find that the Vesper antiphons of January 1 pretty well sum up my whole unashamedly feminine attitude:

> For, ah, who can express
> How full of bonds and simpleness
> Is God,
> How narrow is He,
> And how the wide, waste field of possibility
> Is only trod
> Straight to his homestead in the human heart,
> And all his art
> Is as the babe's that wins his Mother to repeat
> Her little song so sweet. (Patmore: *Legem tuam dilexi*)

If the book of Proverbs proclaims that from the foundation of the earth Divine Wisdom was at play in God's presence, at play everywhere in the world, delighting to be with the sons of men, the Gospels show him playing in his Mother's presence and finding a special delight in the daughters of men. Have you noticed—yes, of course you have—the sparkling freshness that our Lady, in figure and substance, brings to the story of our Lord's incarnation and birth? The antiphons of January 1 are saturated with it. She becomes poetry personified. Hers is the bridal bed and mystic marriage; her divine fruitfulness the flowering of Aaron's rod and the heavenly bedewing of Gideon's fleece; her virginity the sealed fountain, the enclosed garden; she is cedar, rose, honeycomb, perfume, spices. By extension the women in the Gospels introduce at once an atmosphere of joyful relaxation: their children play with our Lord, and they give him not only physical but spiritual comfort as well. Their feminine instinct responds to him with an insight that is subtle, quick, spirited, and unfaltering in the very faith he had come on earth to seek. How many poets have told the story of King Cophetua and the beggar-maid?... Shakespeare, Ben Jonson, Tennyson, Patmore, all retell the legend of the King who looked through his window and fell in love with the beggar-maid and married her. I'm not sure that it isn't the story of every nun's vocation:

> Bare-footed came the beggar maid
> Before the king Cophetua.

The incident is reflected in all our Lord's dealings with women: the Creator craves to become captive as it were to his creature, to the small, the truly humble, the insignificant—our Lady, Martha and Mary, the women he healed, the prostitutes who were, so St. Matthew tells us, among the first to believe in him. My favorite episode is the dialogue between our Lord and the Sidonian woman (Mt. 15:22) which has so much in common with our Lady at Cana. Our Lord's relationship with them reveals that he is really fully human, he can tease, say outrageous things with a poker face and twinkling eye in order to provoke his partner to go one better, and I'm quite sure that it all ended in delighted laughter: I think that the Sidonian woman, who was no lady, probably wagged her finger at him. Both she and our Lady were so unafraid of the Infinite God that they could daringly ignore him and go over his head: each knew perfectly well that he couldn't refuse, and each got exactly what she wanted.

My special love of the Sidonian woman may perhaps derive from a childhood experience. I was five, and for months had watched my baby sister scream from the pain of a line of abscesses open from throat to ear—*My daughter is grievously troubled.* One day the family doctor said very gently to my mother: "Your baby is dying. Be kind to her. Don't move her. Let her die." No sooner was he gone than children's clothes were being hurled into a travelling-bag and in a flash my elder sister, younger brother, and the year-old child in my mother's arms, were entrained along with me en route for Holywell in North Wales and its famous shrine of St. Winefride, with the wonder-working spring of . . ."pale water, frail water, wild rash and reeling water" which, until the advent of cheap air travel to Lourdes, had been thronged with pilgrims from as early as the twelfth century:

> And not from purple Wales only nor from elmy England,
> But from beyond seas, Erin, France and Flanders, everywhere,
> Pilgrims, still pilgrims, more pilgrims, still more poor pilgrims.

As his poem shows, Gerard Manley Hopkins loved the place. Dr. Johnson who visited it with Mrs. Thrale in 1774 was shocked to find "The bath is completely and indecently open. A woman bathed while we all looked on," he thundered. There was no bathing when my pilgrim group reached the shrine in the late afternoon. It stood, nestling in a deep valley encircled by hills, a gem of late Perpendicular architecture open to the skies and populous with praying pilgrims. A small stout man sat at the turn-stile to receive the trifling entrance fee. "Please, will you take my baby and bathe her in the Well, now, immediately? She's dying," said my mother's urgent voice. "No, Madam.

No bathing is allowed in the afternoon. The times for bathing are men at 7:30 and women and children at 9 o'clock every morning." "But the baby's *dying*. Please put her in the water," she pleaded. Further rebuff. "No, I can't accept the responsibility." "But of course not. I accept the responsibility. I'm her mother. My baby's dying. Please take her into the bath!" With a gesture of mock despair, he capitulated and soon appeared in a bathing suit. With Christlike tenderness he clasped the screaming mite and plunged her three times in honor of the Blessed Trinity into the ice-cold pale green water—it never exceeds 52 degrees and never freezes. *She came and adored him saying, Lord, help me.* Pilgrims dotted everywhere prayed aloud to God, to our Lady, to St. Winefride, until the attendant handed the child back to my mother. No further dressing was ever applied to the wound. It merely healed within a few days as if naturally, and we returned home as though it were the most normal thing in the world:

> on heels of air departing,
> Or they go rich as roseleaves hence that loathsome came hither!

O woman, great is your faith. Be it done as you desire. And her daughter was instantly healed. That daughter was to make a happy marriage and is the joyful mother of children.

In his poem on St. Winefride, Hopkins goes on to speak of gifts greater than physical healing,

> Those dearer, more divine boons whose haven the heart is.

After that, I became very much aware of suffering children. At six, I made my first Holy Communion and with a child's quick eye noticed a mentally-retarded girl clinging to her mother's arm each Sunday at Mass. Now why, I asked myself, had our Lord made her like that and me like this? After studying her through laced fingers, I went home to practice in secret being blind and deaf and witless, asking myself at each point: "Why can I see and hear and think? Our Lord has given me my eyes and ears and he could take them away at any time." This sense of absolute dependence on God has followed me all my life, deepened as I went along by the specific text of Romans 11:33. This formed the *leit-motif* of a highly edifying novel, *Via Dolorosa* by a North Country Curate, picked up at a parish fair when I was eight. How I rolled those cadences round my tongue and savored the list of genitives: "Oh the depth of the riches of the wisdom and of the knowledge of God. How incomprehensible are his judgments and how unsearchable his ways"—and with what joy as hebdomadarian I sang those words in euphonious Latin at Vespers years afterwards!

Perhaps love of Wisdom Incarnate drew me to Blessed Henry Suso's *The Little Book of Eternal Wisdom* during my novitiate. "The sharp dart of love" of *The Cloud* had brought the conscious discovery of the pure prayer of the will as being the only means to reach God as he is. As with many novices, my prayer became the be-all and end-all of life; I foolishly imagined that I'd soon arrive at the glorious summit of the Godhead. Not for me to have to climb into the cleft of the rock covered by God's hand and unable to see his face: leave that to Moses. Needless to add, the Ascent of the Great Above was all of a sudden changed into the Descent of the Great Below, and Divine Wisdom's warning to Henry Suso of light turning to darkness, barrenness of heart, and suffering of mind and body, sounded a very personal note: "You will never arrive at my naked Divinity except by breaking through my suffering humanity." And this brings me naturally to the feast of the Dedication of the Church, symbol of the building and adornment of the temple of one's own soul. We sing in the Vesper hymn:

> Tunsionibus pressuris
> Expoliti lapides.

Only with the cutting edge and hard blows of chisel and mallet, and the jointing and cement of prayer are the living stones cut, polished, and built into the spiritual house to "be a holy priesthood and offer spiritual sacrifices acceptable to God through Jesus Christ" (1 Pt. 2:5).

The contemplative life is not, and is not meant to be, a primrose path of dalliance; it is a Via dolorosa even though, to keep a correct balance, one freely admits the truth of Blake's

> Joy and Woe are woven fine
> A Clothing for the Soul divine
> Under every grief and pine
> Runs a joy with silken twine.

On the very eve of his Passion, our Lord spoke of his abounding joy: the two are by no means incompatible. He was moving by painful steps to Gethsemane and the final crux of obedience. Experience teaches that sooner or later every monk and nun will have to face this acid test of obedience to the Father's will. More and more have I realized that obedience was the one bitter lesson that our Lord as Man had to learn. Of all the translations of Heb. 5:8 I like best R. A. Knox's: "Son of God though he was, he learned obedience in the school of suffering." Poverty in the sense of destitution is pretty well non-existent in monastic life; deprivation of family joys demanded by virginity often goes almost unnoticed; but—obedience? Whatever the trial however, God is there all the time, and so often it is the liturgy which supplies the antidote to the bitterness that can be overwhelming on the natural plane. My favorite Collect, now allotted to the ninth Sunday of the Year, has proved a life-line: *Deus, cujus providentia in sui dispositione non fallitur*...whatever his ordinances, God's providence never makes a mistake. The theme is closely linked to the depth of the riches of the wisdom and of the knowledge of God.

At this point, I find I have reached page ten of the type-
script you asked for, and I suspect the sheets are longer
than you bargained for, so may I conclude by making the
vision of Julian of Norwich my own:

> See! I am God: see! I am in all things: see! I do all things: see! I
> lift never mine hands off my works, nor ever shall, without
> end: see! I lead all things to the end I ordained it to from
> without beginning, by the same Might, Wisdom and Love
> whereby I made it. How should any thing be amiss?

WHO DO YOU SAY THAT I AM?

Basil Pennington, OCSO
*(Monk of St. Joseph's Abbey,
Spencer, Massachusetts)*

When I have been privileged to share some thoughts on the Christ-life with my sisters and brothers in Christ, I have often pointed out that there are three kinds of sacred reading we want to practice in our Christian life. There is *sacred study* which is aimed primarily at forming our minds, giving us knowledge and understanding of the Revelation. There is *motivational* or *inspirational reading* meant to incline our wills to live in accord with the fullness of revealed reality. And there is *lectio divina*, or that reading in which we seek the experience of God himself.

When we hear this word addressed to us: Who do you say that I am? I think our first impulse is to seek a response from the first source, our sacred study. In fact, perhaps without even being conscious of it, we tend to transform the question into our Lord's first question: Who do men say that I am? We like to keep things at a safe distance—out there. What do others think: the theologians, the saints and mystics, the popes and councils? But persistently our Lord confronts us with his second question: Who do *you* say that I am? He is not much interested in a response we have gained from sacred study. Nor is anyone else. He wants us to get in touch with our own experience of him. And that is what others want us to share with them, the fruit of our *lectio*. This is a sharing of living faith, the kind of sharing that builds up faith, that edifies in the strictest sense of the word. That is the kind of sharing we want from our priests when they break for us the Bread of the Word in their homilies. How often we are left hungering!

Who do you say that I am? Who does my being say that he is? It *is* my being, for nothing less than my whole being can adequately respond to him. But precisely because this is the case any attempt at verbal articulation of a response whether it be to him in prayer or to others in faith sharing is, indeed, very unsatisfying, betraying in its incompleteness.

Who do you say that I am? My response is sitting at his feet, listening with my whole being. It is standing before him in awed stupidity. It is an incoherent litany of names: God, Father, Lord, Master, Savior, Beloved, Love, My All, You—and each one of them and all of them a distraction and a betrayal.

Who do you say that I am? Mercy upon mercy upon mercy upon mercy. Mercy without end. You are mercy. Love responds to what is; mercy loves what is not and makes it to be. He makes me to be—at each moment—calling me forth from nothingness, sharing with me something of his own divine being, goodness, and beauty. "You are all gods."

Who do you say that I am? You are a man of flesh and blood and guts, like me. You have a big nose; you smell of the Orient; you are Jewish. And all my prejudices get in the way. Heal them, O Lord, heal them. Clean them out. For I can't love you until I love every Jew as myself. Yes, you are a Jew. Did my family, so loving, realize that when they unconsciously bred into me my prejudices? You are a Jew, and yet you are every man. You are the Black, the Hispanic, the poor, the handicapped—all those who touch exposed nerves in my psyche. Heal me through and through, Lord, so that I can truly love you.

Who do you say that I am? I know the catechism answers and more besides. You are the Son of God, one with the Father, the Only-Begotten, One Person with two natures, the God-Man and Savior. I believe all this. But who are you?

I enter the church and my being is drawn irresistibly to

the Host hidden in the red marble tabernacle in the blue and gold niche. Why is this? How did I know since my earliest youth that you are the Host? The theologians will tell me it is a connatural sense coming from the operation of the gifts, the Holy Spirit giving me an instinct for the divine that lies hidden. I believe. Thank you, Lord, for being Host, for the banquet of Body and Blood, for your gracious hospitality.

You are Jesus, the Nazarene, the Son of Mary. I know your Mother. She is my mother, too. You gave her to me. She has taught me a lot about you as I have day after day, decade after decade, told her beads.

Who do you say that I am? I wish, like Thomas, I could say in all truth: You are my God and my All. There are ecstatic moments when I can and do say that. But most of the time the world and the flesh have their sordid claim upon corners of my heart. Lord, heal me and set me free.

Who do you say that I am? I ponder now. And I want to say no more. Words are sordid and cheap. We can use them with so much hollowness. Not everyone who says: Lord, Lord, will enter into the Kingdom. And I *do* want to enter in.

Who do you say that I am? Jesus! Perhaps that says it all. Jesus, my all too human, absolutely divine, ever present Savior.

Who do I say that you are? You are you! What more? And that is enough for me and more than enough. You.

Word and Spirit, 6 — 1984
On Historical Monasticism

To reserve your copy, order from:

St. Bede's Publications
Box 132
Still River, Massachusetts 01467

Still available: Word and Spirit, 1 — 1979
In honor of Saint Basil the Great

Word and Spirit, 2 — 1980
In honor of Saints Benedict and Scholastica

Word and Spirit, 3 — 1981
On the Holy Spirit and on Prayer

Word and Spirit, 4 — 1982
Dedicated to St. Teresa of Avila

Standing orders available

GENERAL THEOLOGICAL SEMINARY
NEW YORK

DATE DUE